This series is dedicated to my late father Thomas L. Brant (1962-2007), without whom I would have never gained my passion for Civil War history.

Table of Contents

Introduction 3
Acknowledgements 5
Fort Sumter, South Carolina 6
Kanawha Valley Campaign, West Virginia 9
Philippi, West Virginia 11
Big Bethel, Virginia 12
Booneville, Missouri 13
Carthage, Missouri 14
Rich Mountain Campaign, West Virginia 16
First Manassas (Bull Run) Campaign, Virginia 19
Wilson's Creek (Springfield or Oak Hills), Missouri 31
Kessler's Cross-Lanes (Cross-Lanes, Summerville), West Virginia 35
Hatteras Expedition, North Carolina 36
Dry Wood Creek (Fort Scott), Missouri 37
Carnifex Ferry, West Virginia 39
Cheat Mountain Campaign, West Virginia 41
Lewinsville, Virginia 44
Siege of Lexington, Missouri 45
Liberty (Blue Mills Landing), Missouri 49
Romney (Hanging Rock), West Virginia 50
Greenbrier River, West Virginia 51
Santa Rosa Island, Florida 53
Fredericktown and Ironton, Missouri 54
Ball's Bluff, Virginia 56
Camp Wildcat (Rockcastle Hills), Kentucky 57
Belmont, Missouri 58
Port Royal (Fort's Beauregard and Walker), South Carolina 62
Ivy Mountain (Piketown), Kentucky 65
Pensacola (Fort Pickens), Florida 66
Camp Alleghany (Buffalo Mountain), West Virginia 68
Rowlett's Station (Mumfordsville, Woodsonville), Kentucky 69
Dranesville, Virginia 70
Bibliography 71
Index 82

Introduction

When I was around eight years old, I was a typical preteen boy, in that virtually all of my enthusiasm was devoted to dinosaurs and superheroes. Then my late father introduced me to his lifelong passion, the American Civil War. I was hooked to say the least, and tried to get my hands on as many Civil War related books and magazines as possible. I also made it my goal to convince everyone I knew that our road trips and vacations be to Civil War battlefields. Then in the 4th grade, a new book sparked a change in the way in which I viewed the Civil War.

There was something in this new book, edited by Time Life Books and titled *Echoes of Glory: Illustrated Atlas of the Civil War,* that I had never seen before some of the major battles covered in the book also included something called the order of battle. How I came to be aware of such a book was purely happenstance, as well as through my 4th grade teacher's awareness of my passion for the Civil War. She made my mother aware of a book on the Civil War available for sale in my elementary school's office. Mom bought the book for me and I was floored; this book had everything! It had photos, text detailing major battles, and maps, as well as the aforementioned orders of battle.

For reasons unknown these order of battle charts fascinated me like nothing else and I was eager to learn as much about them as humanly possible. Alas, *Echoes of Glory* did not contain the organizational charts of every battle covered within, so with the assistance of my maternal grandparents I got a library card and discovered Johnson and Buell's *Battles and Leaders of the Civil War* series. Here I found even more detailed orders of battle. Around this time I also realized that most of the Civil War books devoted to individual campaign studies contained order of battle charts in their appendices; this led me to buying and borrowing as many Civil War books as possible. My ever growing fascination with orders of battle resulted in my handwriting all of this organizational data down in notebooks, my goal being a personal collection of all the major orders of battle of the American Civil War.

With the discovery of the treasure troves that are *The Official Records*, *Dyer's Compendium,* as well as more contemporary works such as Welcher's *The Union Army* set and F. Ray Sibley's *The Confederate Order of Battle Volume 1: The Army of Northern Virginia,* my vision began to seem possible. Over the past twenty years I have worked on and off on this project to produce a 600+ page rough outline of my complete project.

For the project to be more accessible to publishers, readers, and researchers, I concluded that it would be necessary to split the work into multiple volumes. What you hold in your hands is the meticulously researched first volume in what I hope will be the beginning of this project being fully realized. This work is by no means the final say on this subject; there have been order of battle books that cater to specific armies or one specific side or theater of the conflict. However, I do believe this project to be the definitive presentation of organizational data for BOTH Union and Confederate armies and the major conflicts in which they were engaged.

I believe that orders of battle are an integral piece in understanding Civil War combat. The presentation of the command structure not only shows the units and commanders engaged in a particular battle but the ebb and flow of action as represented by command changes in the midst of combat. Not only are command changes, due to death, wounds, capture, illness, or a litany of other reasons, represented in this work; but also noted, when available, are the circumstances concerning a particular change. There were also a number of instances where gaps existed in the historical record with regard to the aforementioned command changes. One of my goals in creating this work was to attempt to fill those gaps. I feel that for the most part I succeeded in this goal through a combination of utilizing recently discovered sources as well as deductive and inductive reasoning. It is my hope that historians, both professional and amateur, genealogists, and even war gamers will find these volumes both useful and fascinating and enjoy these volumes as much as I enjoyed creating them.

-AMB: April 2016

Acknowledgements

While this work was largely an independent effort, the numerous sources included in my research were an indispensable part of my work and research. I would like to thank the authors of every single primary and secondary source I have utilized for your contributions to my research. I am indebted to your hard work and dedication. I would also like to thank Sarah Martin, Park Guide at Fort Sumter National Monument, for helping me make sense of the forces involved in the fight there.

Additionally, I would be remiss if I did not acknowledge my family and extended family/friends both past and present for their constant inspiration, support, and patience throughout the entire process. I also wish to extend special thanks to my wonderfully patient and supportive girlfriend Racheal, for both constant inspiration and for letting me use her laptop for this project during the period when mine crashed.

To everyone mentioned, I wish to extend my gratitude and love for everything you have done for me. It is to every one of you that this work is dedicated.

-AMB: April 2016

Fort Sumter, South Carolina[1]
April 12-13, 1861

Union Forces

Garrison of Fort Sumter (1st U.S. Artillery)
Major Robert Anderson

Engineer Company: Captain John G. Foster
E, 1st United States Artillery: Captain Abner Doubleday
H, 1st United States Artillery: Captain Truman Seymour

Confederate Forces
Brigadier General Pierre G. T. Beauregard

Morris Island[2]
Brigadier General James Simons

Artillery[3]
Lieutenant Colonel Wilmot G. DeSaussure

<u>Cummings Point Batteries</u>: Major Peter F. Stevens
Palmetto Guard: Captain George B. Cuthbert
Palmetto Guard Detachment plus Cadets from Citadel Academy: Captain John P. Thomas[4]
<u>Trapier Battery</u>: Captain John Gadsden King[5]
<u>Channel Batteries</u>:
Wee Nee Riflemen: Captain John G. Pressley[6]
Columbia Artillery: Captain Allen J. Green[7]
German Artillery: Captain Carsten Nohrden[8]

---

[1] Robert U. Johnson and Clarence C. Buel, ends, *Battles and Leaders of the Civil War Volume 1*, (New York, 1887-88), 81; Abner Doubleday, *Reminiscences of Forts Sumter and Moultrie in 1860-61*, (Harper and Brothers, 1876), 179-84.

[2] For commands on Morris Island see: *The War of the Rebellion: A Compilation of the Official Records of the Union and Confederate Armies* (Washington D.C. 1880-1891), *Series I, Vol. I*, 33-34, 37-39. From this point on all Official Records citations will be referred to as OR

[3] *OR Series I Vol. I*, 43-49, 54-58

[4] , Robert S. Seigler, *South Carolina's Military Organizations During the War Between the States, Volume. 4*, (Charleston: The History Press, 2008), 96

[5] Seigler, *South Carolina Vol. 4*, 141

[6] Seigler, *South Carolina Vol. 4*, 249

[7] Seigler, *South Carolina Vol. 4*, 187

[8] Seigler, *South Carolina Vol. 4*, 265

Infantry[9]

17th South Carolina State Militia: Colonel John Cunningham[10]
1st South Carolina: Colonel Johnson Hagood[11]
1st South Carolina Provisional Army: Colonel Maxcy Gregg[12]
2nd (Palmetto Regiment) South Carolina: Colonel Joseph B. Kershaw[13]

James Island

Fort Johnson Batteries: Captain George S. James

Sullivan's Island[14]
Brigadier General Richard G. M. Dunovant

Sullivan's Island Artillery[15]
Lieutenant Colonel Roswell S. Ripley

Five Gun Battery: Captain Samuel Y. Tupper[16]
Ironclad Floating Battery: Lieutenant Joseph A. Yates[17]
Point Battery: Captain John R. Hamilton
The Enfilade Battery & Mortar Battery No. 1: Captain James H. Hallonquist
    Enfilade Battery: Lieutenant Jacob Valentine
    Mortar Battery No. 1: Lieutenant Ormsby Blanding and Lieutenant David G. Fleming[18]
Fort Moultrie Batteries: Captain William R. Calhoun
    Sumter Battery: Lieutenant. Alfred M. Rhett
    Channel Battery: Lieutenant Thomas M. Wagner
    Oblique Battery: Lieutenant. Charles W. Parker[19]
Mortar Battery No. 2 and Maffit Channel Battery: Captain William Butler
Mount Pleasant Battery: Captain Robert Martin

---

[9] Clement A. Evans, ed., *Confederate Military History Volume 5*, (Atlanta: Confederate Publishing Company, 1899), 16. Hereafter referred to as *CMH*
[10] Seigler, *South Carolina Vol. 4*, 238
[11] Seigler, *South Carolina Vol. 1*, 45-79
[12] Seigler, *South Carolina Vol. 1*, 81-110
[13] Seigler, *South Carolina Vol. 1*, 111-32
[14] For commanders on Sullivan's Island see, *OR Series I, Vol. I*, 33-34, 35-37
[15] *OR Series I, Vol. I*, 39-43, 50-54
[16] Seigler, *South Carolina Vol. 4*, 266
[17] Seigler, *South Carolina Vol. 4*, 137
[18] Seigler, *South Carolina Vol. 4*, 137, 139
[19] Seigler, *South Carolina Vol 4*, 140

Infantry

1st South Carolina State Militia Rifles: Colonel James Johnston Pettigrew[20]
1st South Carolina Regulars: Colonel Richard H. Anderson[21]

Cavalry

Charleston Light Dragoons: Captain Benjamin H. Rutledge[22]

Unattached Cavalry[23]

German Hussars: Captain Theodore Cordes
Rutledge Mounted Riflemen: Captain Cleland K. Huger

---

[20] Evans ed, *CMH Vol. 5*, 5, 16; Seigler, *South Carolina Vol 4*, 225-31
[21] Evans ed, *CMH Vol. 5*, 16; Seigler, *South Carolina Vol 4*, 135
[22] Evans ed, *CMH Vol. 5*, 16
[23] Evans ed, *CMH Vol. 5*, 5

Kanawha Valley Campaign, West Virginia
June-July, 1861
(Includes Engagements at Red House [July 12], Barboursville (Mud River) [July 14] and Scary Creek (Scarytown) [July 17])

Union Forces[24]
Brigadier General Jacob D. Cox

1st Kentucky: Colonel James V. Guthrie (w)
    Lieutenant Colonel David A. Enyart[25]
2nd Kentucky: Colonel William E. Woodruff (c)
    Lieutenant Colonel George W. Neff (c)
    Lieutenant Colonel Thomas D. Sedgwick[26]
11th Ohio: Colonel Charles DeVilliers (c)
    Lieutenant Colonel Joseph W. Frizell[27]
12th Ohio: Colonel John W. Lowe[28]
21st Ohio: Colonel Jesse S. Norton (w&c)
    Lieutenant Colonel James M. Neibling[29]
Independent Company Ohio Cavalry: Captain John S. George
Independent Ohio Artillery Battery: Captain Charles S. Cotter
Independent Ohio Artillery Battery: Captain William S. Williams[30]
1st Kentucky Independent Battery: Captain Seth J. Simmonds

Confederate Forces[31]
Brigadier General Henry A. Wise

22nd Virginia: Colonel Christopher Q. Tompkins
    Lieutenant Colonel George S. Patton (w)
    Colonel Christopher Q. Tompkins[32]

---

[24] Frederick Phisterer, *Statistical Record of the Armies of the United States*, (New York: Charles Scribner's Sons, 1883), 85; Terry Lowry, *The Battle of Scary Creek: Military Operations in the Kanawha Valley April-July 1861*, (Charleston, W.Va.: Quarrier Press, 1998), 237

[25] Guthrie wounded in the hand June 30, Roger D. Hunt, *Colonels in Blue: Indiana, Kentucky, and Tennessee*, (McFarland, 2014), 160; Lowry, *Scary Creek*, 41, 143

[26] Both Woodruff and Neff were captured July 17, Lowry, *Scary Creek*, 235, 143

[27] DeVilliers captured at Scary Creek, Lowry, *Scary Creek*, 235; *Official Roster of the Soldiers of the State of Ohio in the War of the Rebellion 1861-1866 Vol. 2*, (The Werner Company: Akron, 1893), 321. Hereafter Referred to as *Ohio*

[28] Lowry, *Scary Creek*, 38

[29] Norton wounded in the thigh at Scary Creek, and subsequently captured. Lowry, *Scary Creek*, 235. See, Lowry, *Scary Creek*, 141-43 for Neibling

[30] Consolidated with Cotter's Battery July 2, Lowry, *Scary Creek*, 237

[31] Lowry, *Scary Creek*, xii

36th Virginia: Lieutenant Colonel John McCausland[33]
59th Virginia (Companies A & B): Captain Obadiah Jennings Wise[34]
120th Virginia Militia: Colonel Joseph J. Mansfield (mw)
                Lieutenant Colonel A. B. McGinnis[35]
Virginia (Kanawha Artillery) Battery: Captain John P. Hale[36]

Cavalry: Captain Albert G. Jenkins (w)[37]
Cabell County Border Rangers: Captain Albert G. Jenkins
Sandy Rangers: Captain James M. Corns
Fayette Rangers: Captain William Tyree
Kanawha Rangers: Captain Charles I. Lewis

27th Brigade Virginia Militia: Brigadier General Alfred Beckley[38]
119th Virginia Militia: Colonel William F. Kemble
126th Virginia Militia: Colonel Edward Campbell
129th Virginia Militia: Colonel John De Jernatt
142nd Virginia Militia: Colonel Samuel B. Woods
184th Virginia Militia: Lieutenant Colonel Joseph Caldwell
187th Virginia Militia: Colonel Ezekiel S. Miller
190th Virginia Militia: Colonel William N. Henderson

---

[32] Patton commanded the regiment at Scary Creek where he was wounded in the left shoulder, see, Lowry, *Scary Creek*, 21, 234; Terry Lowry, *September Blood: The Battle of Carnifex Ferry*, (Charleston, W.Va.: Pictorial Histories Publishing Company, 1988), 33; Lee A. Wallace Jr. *A Guide to Virginia Military Organizations 1861-1865*, (H.E. Howard, Inc., 1986), 104-05; Stewart Sifakis, *Compendium of the Confederate Armies: Virginia*, (New York: Facts on File Inc., 1992), 200-01. Hereafter referred to as *Confederate*

[33] Lowry, *Scary Creek*, 17; Wallace, *Virginia*, 118-19; Sifakis, *Confederate: Virginia*, 223-24

[34] Wallace, *Virginia*, 136-37, 52

[35] Mansfield mortally wounded at Barboursville "in the back and died three days later." Lowry, *Scary Creek*, 239. McGinnis listed as Mansfield's successor see Bobby Lee Arrington, "Confederate Units Militia," *West Virginia The Other History*. Accessed December 6, 2014. https://sites.google.com/site/wvotherhistory/confederate-units-militia. Note: This site lists Lee A. Wallace Jr., *A Guide to Virginia Military Organizations, 1861-1865*, (Virginia Civil War Commission, 1964) and James Carter Linger, *Confederate Military Units of West Virginia*, (Privately Published, 2002) as the sources for their information.

[36] Lowry, *Scary Creek*, 18

[37] Slightly wounded in the head at Scary Creek, Lowry, *Scary Creek*, 45, 234;

[38] OR Series I, Vol. II, 951-52; Wallace, *Virginia*, 271-73; Bobby Lee Arrington, "Confederate Units Militia," *West Virginia The Other History*. Accessed December 6, 2014. https://sites.google.com/site/wvotherhistory/confederate-units-militia. Note: This site lists Lee A. Wallace Jr., *A Guide to Virginia Military Organizations, 1861-1865*, (Virginia Civil War Commission, 1964) and James Carter Linger, *Confederate Military Units of West Virginia*, (Privately Published, 2002) as the sources for their information

Philippi, West Virginia
June 3, 1861

Union Forces[39]
Brigadier General Thomas A. Morris

<u>Left Column</u>: Colonel Benjamin F. Kelly (w)[40]
9th Indiana (9 companies): Colonel Robert H. Milroy
16th Ohio (6 companies): Colonel John Irvine
1st West Virginia (6 companies): Colonel Benjamin F. Kelly

<u>Right Column</u>: Colonel Ebenezer Dumont
6th Indiana (6 companies): Colonel Thomas T. Crittenden
7th Indiana (8 companies): Colonel Ebenezer Dumont
14th Ohio (5 companies): Colonel James B. Steedman
15th Ohio (3 companies): Lieutenant Colonel Moses R. Dickey

<u>Artillery</u>: Colonel Frederick W. Lander & Lieutenant Colonel Stephen B. Sturges[41]
D, 1st Ohio Light Artillery: Captain Percy W. Rice[42]
F, 1st Ohio Light Artillery: Captain Dennis Kenny Jr.[43]

Confederate Forces[44]
Colonel George A. Porterfield

9 companies Virginia Militia: Captain Albert G. Reger
5 companies Virginia Militia Cavalry: Captain William K. Jenkins

---

[39] *OR Series I, Vol. II*, 66-67.
[40] Kelly was wounded by "a pistol shot in the right breast." *OR, Series I, Vol. II,,* 68
[41] Lander had overall command of the artillery, *OR Series I, Vol. II*, 67; Eva Margaret Carnes ed., *Centennial History of the Philippi Covered Bridge, 1852-1952*, (Barbour County Historical Society, 1952), 82; *Ohio Vol. 1*, 712
[42] *Ohio Vol. 1*, 717
[43] *Ohio Vol. 1*, 718
[44] *OR, Series I, Vol. II*, 72; Carnes ed., *Philippi Covered Bridge*, 82

Big Bethel, Virginia
June 10, 1861

Union Forces [45]
Brigadier General Ebenezer W. Pierce

1st New York: Colonel William H. Allen
2nd New York: Colonel Joseph B. Carr
3rd New York: Colonel Frederick Townsend
5th New York: Colonel Abram Duryea
7th New York: Colonel John E. Bendix
4th Massachusetts: Major Horace O. Whittemore
1st Vermont: Lieutenant Colonel Peter Washburn
B, 2nd United States Artillery (2 guns): Lieutenant John T. Greble (k)[46]

Confederate Forces[47]
Colonel John B. Magruder

1st North Carolina: Colonel Daniel Harvey Hill
3rd (15th) Virginia: Lieutenant Colonel William D. Stuart
Virginia Infantry Battalion: Major Edgar B. Montague
3rd Virginia Cavalry (Companies A, B, and D): Major John Bell Hood[48]

Richmond (1st) Howitzer Battalion: Major George W. Randolph
2nd Company: Captain John Thompson Brown[49]
3rd Company: Captain Robert C. Stanard[50]

---

[45] *OR, Series I, Vol II*, 77-82.
[46] Greble killed by enemy artillery fire while "efficiently and gallantly" defending his guns. *OR Series I, Vol. II*, 80
[47] *OR, Series I, Vol. II*, 93-97.
[48] Wallace, *Virginia*, 42-43
[49] Sifakis, *Confederate: Virginia*, 73-74; F. Ray Sibley Jr., *Confederate Artillery Organizations: An Alphabetical Listing of the Officers and Batteries of the Confederacy 1861-1865*, (Savas Beattie LLC, 2014), 224
[50] Sifakis, *Confederate: Virginia*, 74-75; Sibley, *Confederate Artillery Organizations*, 225

Booneville, Missouri
June 17, 1861

Union Forces[51]
Brigadier General Nathaniel Lyon

1st Missouri: Colonel Francis P. Blair Jr.
2nd Missouri (4 companies): Lieutenant Colonel Frederick Schaefer
2nd United States (1 company): Sergeant William Griffin
2 Unattached Companies United States Recruits: Lieutenant Warren L. Lothrop
F, 2nd United States Artillery: Captain James Totten

Confederate Forces

1st Missouri State Guard Rifles: Colonel John S. Marmaduke[52]

---

[51] *OR Series I, Vol. III*, 12-13; Douglas D. Scott, Thomas D. Thiessen, and Steve J. Dasovich, *The "First" Battle of Boonville, Cooper County, Missouri, June 17, 1861: Archaeological and Historical Investigations* (Missouri Civil War Heritage Foundation, 2009), 21-23

[52] Richard C. Peterson, James E. McGhee, Kip A. Lindberg, and Keith I. Daleen, *Sterling Price's Lieutenants: A Guide to the Officers and Organization of the Missouri State Guard 1861-1865 Revised Edition*, (Independence, Mo.: Two Trails Publishing, 2007), 253-56. Hereafter referred to as *Price's Lieutenants*.

Carthage, Missouri
July 5, 1861

Union Forces[53]
Colonel Franz Sigel

3rd Missouri (9 Companies): Lieutenant. Colonel Francis Hassendeubel & Major Henry Bischoff[54]
5th Missouri (7 Companies): Colonel Charles E. Salomon & Lieutenant. Colonel Christian D. Wolff[55]
<u>Artillery</u>: Major Franz Backof
Four gun Battery: Captain Christian Essig
Four gun Battery: Captain Theodore Wilkins

Confederate Forces[56]
Missouri State Guard
Governor Claiborne F. Jackson

<u>3rd Division</u>: Brigadier General John B. Clark Sr.
1st Missouri State Guard: Colonel John Q. Burbridge[57]
1st Missouri State Guard Cavalry Battalion: Major James P. Major[58]

<u>4th Division</u>: Brigadier General William Y. Slack
1st Missouri State Guard: Colonel John T. Hughes[59]
1st Missouri State Guard Cavalry: Colonel Benjamin A. Rives[60]
1st Missouri State Guard Cavalry Battalion: Major John C. C. Thornton[61]

<u>6th Division</u>: Brigadier General Mosby Monroe Parsons
1st Missouri State Guard: Colonel Joseph Kelly[62]
1st Missouri State Guard Cavalry: Colonel William B. Brown[63]

---

[53] *OR, Series I, Vol. III*, 16-19
[54] Regiment was split into 2 battalions, thus 2 separate commanders. David C. Hinze & Karen Farnham, *The Battle of Carthage: Border War in Southwest Missouri, July 5, 1861*, (Savas Publishing Company, 1997), 122
[55] See Above
[56] *OR, Series I, Vol. III*, 20-37
[57] Peterson et al, *Price's Lieutenants*, 164
[58] Peterson et al, *Price's Lieutenants*, 163
[59] Peterson et al, *Price's Lieutenants*, 203
[60] Peterson et al, *Price's Lieutenants*, 196
[61] Peterson et al, *Price's Lieutenants*, 229-30. From 5th Division.
[62] Peterson et al, *Price's Lieutenants*, 273

1st Missouri State Guard Light Artillery Battery: Captain Henry C. Guibor[64]

8th Division: Brigadier General James S. Rains
1st (Infantry) Brigade: Colonel Richard H. Weightman
1st Missouri State Guard: Lieutenant Colonel Thomas H. Rosser
2nd Missouri State Guard: Colonel John R. Graves
3rd Missouri State Guard: Colonel Edgar V.R. Hurst
4th Missouri State Guard Battalion: Lieutenant Colonel Walter S. O'Kane[65]
5th Missouri State Guard: Colonel James J. Clarkson[66]
2nd (Cavalry) Brigade: Colonel James Cawthorn[67]
1st Missouri State Guard Cavalry (elements): Lieutenant Colonel John W. Martin[68]
2nd Missouri State Guard Cavalry: Lieutenant Colonel James C. McCown
3rd Missouri State Guard Cavalry (Companies A, B, and Part of H): Colonel Robert L.Y. Peyton[69]
4th Missouri State Guard Cavalry: Lieutenant Colonel Benjamin F. Walker[70]
5th Missouri State Guard Cavalry: Colonel Jeremiah C. Cravens[71]
6th Missouri State Guard Cavalry: Lieutenant Colonel John W. Payne[72]
7th Missouri State Guard Cavalry: Lieutenant Colonel Richard A. Baughan[73]
9th Missouri State Guard Cavalry (elements): Lieutenant Colonel Thomas B. Cummings[74]
Lafayette Country Mounted Rifle Company: Captain Joseph O. Shelby[75]
Artillery
1st (Price's Rifles) Missouri State Guard Light Artillery Battery: Captain Hiram M. Bledsoe[76]

---

[63] Commander listed in reports as Ben Brown, however, according to Peterson et al, *Price's Lieutenants*, 31, 194, 258 Ben Brown was inspector general of the 4th Division, and the regiment was commanded by Col William B. Brown
[64] Peterson et al, *Price's Lieutenants*, 285
[65] Peterson et al, *Price's Lieutenants*, 342-46
[66] Peterson et al, *Price's Lieutenants*, 347-51
[67] Peterson et al, *Price's Lieutenants*, 356
[68] Peterson et al, *Price's Lieutenants*, 357-61
[69] Peterson et al, *Price's Lieutenants*, 368-72
[70] Peterson et al, *Price's Lieutenants*, 372-76
[71] Peterson et al, *Price's Lieutenants*, 376-80
[72] Peterson et al, *Price's Lieutenants*, 380-85
[73] Peterson et al, *Price's Lieutenants*, 385
[74] Peterson et al, *Price's Lieutenants*, 390-92
[75] Peterson et al, *Price's Lieutenants*, 408
[76] Peterson et al, *Price's Lieutenants*, 410

Rich Mountain Campaign, West Virginia
July 9-14, 1861
(Includes Engagements at Laurel Hill, Rich Mountain, and Corrick's (Carrick's) Ford

Union Forces[77]
Army of Occupation West Virginia
Brigadier General George B. McClellan

<u>Brigade</u>: Brigadier General William S. Rosecrans[78]
8th Indiana: Colonel William P. Benton
10th Indiana: Colonel Mahlon D. Manson
13th Indiana: Colonel Jeremiah C. Sullivan
17th Ohio: Colonel John M. Connell
19th Ohio: Colonel Samuel Beatty
Independent Ohio Cavalry Company: Captain Henry W. Bursdal[79]

<u>Brigade</u>: Brigadier General Newton Schleich
3rd Ohio: Colonel Isaac H. Morrow
6th Ohio: Colonel William K. Bosley
7th Ohio: Colonel Erastus B. Tyler
14th Indiana: Colonel Nathan Kimball
15th Indiana: Colonel George D. Wagner

<u>Brigade</u>: Colonel Robert L. McCook[80]
4th Ohio: Colonel Lorin Andrews
9th Ohio: Lieutenant Colonel Charles Sondershoff
A, 1st Michigan Light Artillery: Captain Cyrus O. Loomis

<u>Brigade</u>: Brigadier General Thomas A. Morris[81]
6th Indiana: Colonel Thomas T. Crittenden
7th Indiana: Colonel Ebenezer Dumont
9th Indiana: Colonel Robert H. Milroy
14th Ohio: Colonel James B. Steedman

---

[77] Frank J. Welcher, *The Union Army 1861-1865 Organization and Operations Volume 1: The Eastern Theater* (Bloomington and Indianapolis: Indiana University Press, 1989), 1058-1059.; Frederick H. Dyer, *A Compendium of the War of the Rebellion Volume 1: Number and Organization of the Armies of the United States* (New York and London: Thomas Yoseloff Publisher, 1959), 334-35
[78] *OR, Series I, Vol. II,*
[79] *Ohio Vol. 1,* 737
[80] *OR,* Series I, Vol. II, 200.
[81] *OR,* Series I, Vol. II, 218-221

1st Ohio Light Artillery: Colonel James Barnett[82]
A, 1st Ohio Light Artillery: Captain William R. Simmonds
B, 1st Ohio Light Artillery: Captain John G. Mack
C, 1st Ohio Light Artillery: Captain Frederick W. Pelton
D, 1st Ohio Light Artillery: Captain Percy W. White
E, 1st Ohio Light Artillery: Captain Louis Heckman
F, 1st Ohio Light Artillery: Captain Dennis Kenny Jr.

Brigade: Brigadier General Charles W. Hill[83]
5th Ohio: Colonel Samuel H. Dunning
8th Ohio: Colonel Herman G. Depuy
13th Ohio: Colonel William Sooy Smith
15th Ohio: Colonel George W. Andrews
16th Ohio: Colonel John Irvine
18th Ohio: Colonel Timothy R. Stanley
20th Ohio: Colonel Thomas Morton
22nd Ohio: Lieutenant Colonel John A. Turley
A, 1st West Virginia Light Artillery: Captain Philip Daum

Artillery:
G, 4th United States Artillery: Captain Albion P. Howe
I, 4th United States Artillery: Captain Oscar A. Mack

Confederate Forces
Department of Northwestern Virginia[84]
Brigadier General Robert S. Garnett (k)[85]

Rich Mountain: Lieutenant Colonel John Pegram (c) [86]
20th Virginia: Lieutenant Colonel John Pegram[87]
25th Virginia: Lieutenant Colonel Jonathan M. Heck[88]

---

[82] *Ohio Vol. 1*, 711-18
[83] *OR, Series I, Vol. II*, 224-229
[84] *OR, Series I, Vol. II*, 236-244; Evans ed, *CMH Vol. 3,* 45-56.
[85] Killed at Carrick's Ford July 13, 1861. Garnett was shot in the side while ordering his rear guard skirmishers to retire, thus making him the first confederate general killed in the war. Derek Smith, *The Gallant Dead: Union and Confederate Generals Killed in the Civil War*, (Mechanicsburg Pennsylvania: Stackpole Books, 2008), 3.
[86] Pegram elected to surrender his command after being surrounded by enemy forces at Rich Mountain on July 11. Command was paroled except for Pegram who was "refused his parole because he had been an officer in the U. S. Army." *OR Series I, Vol. II*, 254-59, 264-68; Mark M. Boatner III, *The Civil War Dictionary*, (New York: David McKay Company, Inc., 1959), 232
[87] Sifakis, *Confederate: Virginia*, 196; Wallace, *Virginia*, 102
[88] Sifakis, *Confederate: Virginia*, 205-07; Wallace, *Virginia*, 107-09

44th Virginia: Colonel William C. Scott[89]
14th Virginia Cavalry (Company I): Captain Franklin P. Sterrett
DeLagnel's Command (Companies B, D, E of 20th Virginia; Companies A & B of 25th Virginia):
    Captain Julius A. DeLagnel (w)[90]
Virginia (Lynchburg "Lee" Artillery) Battery: Captain Pierce B. Anderson[91]

<u>Laurel Hill</u>: Brigadier General Robert S. Garnett
1st Georgia: Colonel James N. Ramsey
9th Virginia Battalion: Major George W. Hansbrough
23rd Virginia: Colonel William B. Taliaferro
31st Virginia: Lieutenant Colonel William L. Jackson
37th Virginia: Colonel Samuel V. Fulkerson
Virginia Cavalry Squadron: Captain John G. Smith
Virginia Cavalry Squadron: Captain George Jackson
Virginia (Danville Artillery) Battery: Captain Lindsay M. Shumaker[92]

---

[89] Not captured at Rich Mountain, at Beverly, *OR Series I, Vol. II*, 265
[90] Severely wounded in the Battle of Rich Mountain. *OR Series I, Vol. II*, 264; "Captain J. A. De Lagnel no words can express all that should be felt or known about his conduct on that day. After nearly all his cannoneers were either killed or wounded, he continued to load his gun until in the very act of bringing a cartridge from the limber-box to the gun (having then only two men at the gun) he was struck by a minie ball and fell. Fortunately, however, he escaped capture," *OR*, Series I, Vol. II, 270
[91] *OR Series I, Vol. V*, 463
[92] Jennings Cropper Wise, *The Long Arm of Lee or History of the Artillery of the Army of Northern Virginia* (Lynchburg, Va.: J.P. Bell & Company, 1915), 990

First Manassas (Bull Run) Campaign, Virginia
June 18-July 22, 1861
(Includes Engagements at Falling Waters, West Virginia; Blackburn's Ford, & 1st Battle of Manassas (Bull Run), Virginia)

Union Forces
Army of Northeastern Virginia[93]
Brigadier General Irvin McDowell

1st Division: Brigadier General Daniel Tyler
1st Brigade: Colonel Erasmus D. Keyes
2nd Maine: Colonel Charles D. Jameson
1st Connecticut: Colonel George S. Burnham[94]
2nd Connecticut: Colonel Alfred H. Terry
3rd Connecticut: Colonel John L. Chatfield
2nd Brigade: Brigadier General Robert C. Schenck
2nd New York: Colonel George W. B. Tompkins[95]
1st Ohio: Colonel Alexander M. McCook
2nd Ohio: Lieutenant Colonel Rodney Mason[96]
E, 2nd United States Artillery: Captain John Howard Carlisle
3rd Brigade: Colonel William T. Sherman
13th New York: Colonel Isaac F. Quinby
69th New York: Colonel Michael Corcoran (w&c)
    Captain James Kelly[97]
79th New York: Colonel James Cameron (k)
    Lieutenant Colonel Samuel M. Elliott[98]
2nd Wisconsin: Lieutenant Colonel Henry W. Peck[99]
E, 3rd United States Artillery: Captain Romeyn B. Ayres
4th Brigade: Colonel Israel B. Richardson
1st Massachusetts: Colonel Robert Cowdin

---

[93] *B&L Vol. 1*, 194
[94] Connecticut Adjutant General's Office, *Catalogue of Connecticut Volunteer Organizations, (infantry, Cavalry, and Artillery,) in the Service of the United States, 1861-1865*, (Brown and Gross, 1869), 3
[95] Frederick Phisterer, *New York in the War of the Rebellion 1861 to 1865* (J.B. Lyon Company, State Printer, 1912), 2898
[96] *Ohio Vol. 1*, 21
[97] Corcoran wounded in the leg and captured July 21, 1861. See *OR*, Series I, Vol. II, 371-372; Jack D. Welsh, *Medical Histories of Union Generals*, (Kent State University Press, 2005), 77
[98] Cameron shot in the chest and killed "leading his regiment in the charge" July 21, 1861. See *OR*, Series I, Vol. II, 371; Phisterer, *New York*, 2843; Roger D. Hunt, *Colonels in Blue: New York*, (Schiffer Publishing, 2003), 62
[99] Wisconsin Adjutant General's Office, *Roster of Wisconsin Volunteers, War of the Rebellion, 1861-1865. Volume 1*, (Madison: Democrat Printing Company, 1886), 345

12th New York: Colonel Ezra L. Walrath
2nd Michigan: Major Adolphus W. Williams[100]
3rd Michigan: Colonel Daniel McConnell
G, 1st United States Artillery: Lieutenant John Edwards
M, 2nd United States Artillery: Captain Henry J. Hunt

2nd Division: Colonel David Hunter (w)
        Colonel Andrew Porter[101]
<u>1st Brigade</u>: Colonel Andrew Porter
8th New York (Militia): Colonel George Lyons
14th New York (Militia): Colonel Alfred M. Wood (w&c)
        Lieutenant Colonel Edward B. Fowler[102]
27th New York: Colonel Henry W. Slocum (w)
        Major Joseph J. Bartlett[103]
United States Infantry Battalion (8 companies): Major George Sykes
United States Marine Corps Battalion: Major John G. Reynolds
5th United States Cavalry (7 companies): Major Innis N. Palmer
D, 5th United States Artillery: Captain Charles Griffin
<u>2nd Brigade</u>: Colonel Ambrose E. Burnside
2nd New Hampshire: Colonel Gilman Marston (w)
        Lieutenant Colonel Frank S. Fiske[104]
1st Rhode Island: Major Joseph P. Balch[105]
2nd Rhode Island: Colonel John S. Slocum (k)
        Lieutenant Colonel Frank Wheaton[106]
71st New York: Colonel Henry P. Martin[107]
2nd Rhode Island Battery: Captain William H. Reynolds

---

[100] *Record of service of Michigan volunteers in the civil war, 1861-1865. Pub by authority of the Senate and House of representatives of the Michigan Legislature under the direction of Brig. Gen. Geo. H. Brown, adjutant general. Volume 2*, (Ihling Bros. & Everard, Printers, no year given), 2

[101] Hunter, wounded in the neck by a shell fragment July 21, 1861, command of the division fell to Col Andrew Porter. *OR*, Series I, Vol. II, 334; Welsh, *Medical Histories of Union Generals*, 179

[102] Wood wounded in the right hip and captured July 21, Hunt, *Colonels in Blue: New York*, 310

[103] Slocum was wounded July 21 and replaced by Major Joseph J. Bartlett "During our retreat Colonel Slocum received a wound from a musket ball in the right thigh, which rendered it necessary for him to retire from the field, which he did, placing the command in my hands." *OR* Series I, Vol. II, 389.

[104] "Marston was badly wounded in the shoulder" on July 21. See *OR* Series I, Vol. II, 399 for Marston's wounding and Fisk's succession. *Revised Register of the Soldiers and Sailors of New Hampshire in the War of Rebellion 1861-1866*, (Concord: Ira C. Evans Public Printer, 1895), 49

[105] *Annual report of the adjutant general of Rhode Island and Providence Plantations, for the year 1865*, (Providence: E.L. Freeman and Son, 1893-95), 10

[106] Slocum shot in the head and killed July 21, Roger D. Hunt, *Colonels in Blue: The New England States*, (Schiffer, 2001), 193

[107] Phisterer, *New York*, 691

3rd Division: Colonel Samuel P. Heintzelman (w)[108]
1st Brigade: Colonel William B. Franklin
5th Massachusetts: Colonel Samuel C. Lawrence[109]
11th Massachusetts: Colonel George Clark Jr.
1st Minnesota: Colonel Willis A. Gorman
4th Pennsylvania: Colonel John F. Hartranft
I, 1st United States Artillery: Captain James B. Ricketts (w&c)
                             Lieutenant Edmund Kirby[110]
2nd Brigade: Colonel Orlando B. Willcox (w&c)
              Colonel John Henry Hobart Ward[111]
11th New York: Lieutenant Colonel Noah L. Farnham (mw)
                 Major Charles M. Leoser[112]
38th New York: Colonel John Henry Hobart Ward
                Lieutenant Colonel Addison Farnsworth
1st Michigan: Major Alonzo F. Bidwell[113]
4th Michigan: Colonel Dwight A. Woodbury
D, 2nd United States Artillery: Captain Richard Arnold
3rd Brigade: Colonel Oliver O. Howard
3rd Maine: Major Henry G. Staples
4th Maine: Colonel Hiram G. Berry
5th Maine: Colonel Mark H. Dunnell[114]
2nd Vermont: Colonel Henry Whiting

4th Division: Brigadier General Theodore Runyon[115]
Militia
1st New Jersey: Colonel Adolphus J. Johnson[116]
2nd New Jersey: Colonel Henry M. Baker[117]

---

[108] Wounded July 21, "in the arm while leading his division into action." *OR*, Series I, Vol. II, 323. Heintzelman did not leave the field after being wounded. Frank Moore ed. *The Portrait Gallery of the War Civil, Military and Naval: A Biographical Record*. (New York: D. Van Nostrand Publisher, 1865), 179

[109] *Massachusetts Soldiers, Sailors, and Marines in the Civil War, Vol. 1*, (Norwood Press, 1931), 270

[110] Ricketts wounded 4 times and captured July 21, 1861. See *OR*, Series I, Vol. II, 410; Welsh, *Medical Histories of Union Generals*, 279

[111] Willcox "received a frightful wound in the right arm from an exploding shell ; his horse was shot under him and fell, and he, faint from loss of blood, was taken prisoner by the rebels, together with two of his cap tains," Moore ed. *The Portrait Gallery of the War Civil,* 160; See *OR* Series I, Vol. II, 410 for Ward

[112] Farnham mortally wounded in the head July 21, died August 14, Phisterer, *New York*, 1862, 1867; Hunt, *Colonels in Blue: New York*, 121

[113] *Michigan, Vol. 1*, 1

[114] William E.S. Whitman and Charles H. True, *Maine in the War for the Union*,(Nelson Dingley Jr. & Co. Publishers, 1865), 111

[115] Not engaged in battle, ordered to function as army's reserve and guard forces. See *OR*, Series I, Vol. II, 304

[116] *Records of officers and men of New Jersey in the Civil War, 1861-1865 Volume 1*, (Trenton: John L. Murphy Steam Book and Job Printer, 1876), 15

3rd New Jersey: Colonel William Napton
4th New Jersey: Colonel Matthew Miller Jr.
<u>Volunteers</u>
1st New Jersey: Colonel William R. Montgomery
2nd New Jersey: Colonel George W. McLean
3rd New Jersey: Colonel George W. Taylor
41st New York: Colonel Leopold Von Gilsa

5th Division: Colonel Dixon S. Miles[118]
<u>1st Brigade</u>: Colonel Louis Blenker
8th New York: Lieutenant Colonel Julius Stahel
29th New York: Colonel Adolph W. Von Steinwehr
39th New York: Colonel Frederick G. D'Utassy
27th Pennsylvania: Colonel Max Einstein
A, 2nd United States Artillery: Captain John C. Tidball
8th New York Militia Battery: Captain Charles Bookwood
<u>2nd Brigade</u>: Colonel Thomas A. Davies
16th New York: Lieutenant Colonel Samuel Marsh
18th New York: Colonel William A. Jackson[119]
31st New York: Colonel Calvin E. Pratt
32nd New York: Colonel Roderick Matheson
G, 2nd United States Artillery: Lieutenant Oliver D. Greene

<u>McCunn's Brigade</u>: Colonel John H. McCunn[120]
15th New York: Colonel John M. Murphy[121]
25th New York: Colonel James E. Kerrigan[122]
26th New York: Colonel William H. Christian
37th New York: Lieutenant Colonel John Burke[123]

Army of Pennsylvania
Major General Robert Patterson

1st Division: Major General George Cadwalader

---

[117] *New Jersey Vol. 1*, 28
[118] In reserve at Centreville and not fully engaged with the enemy. See *OR*, Series I, Vol. II, 315
[119] Phisterer, *New York*, 1947
[120] Not engaged in battle, ordered to join McDowell's army as reinforcements on July 21. See *OR*, Series I, Vol. II, 750-751
[121] Phisterer, *New York*, 1651
[122] Phisterer, *New York*, 2013
[123] Phisterer, *New York*, 2160

1st Brigade: Colonel George H. Thomas[124]
6th Pennsylvania: Colonel James Nagle
21st Pennsylvania: Colonel John F. Ballier
23rd Pennsylvania: Colonel Charles P. Dare
E, 1st United States Artillery: Captain Abner Doubleday[125]
3rd Brigade: Brigadier General Edward C. Williams[126]
7th Pennsylvania: Colonel William H. Irwin
8th Pennsylvania: Colonel Anthony H. Emley[127]
10th Pennsylvania: Colonel Sullivan A. Meredith
20th Pennsylvania (Scott Legion): Colonel William H. Gray
4th Brigade: Colonel Dixon S. Miles
        Colonel Henry C. Longenecker[128]
9th Pennsylvania: Colonel Henry C. Longenecker
        Lieutenant Colonel William H. H. Hangen[129]
13th Pennsylvania: Colonel Thomas A. Rowley
16th Pennsylvania: Colonel Thomas A. Zeigler
2nd and 3rd United States: Major Oliver L. Shepherd

2nd Division: Major General William H. Keim
2nd Brigade: Brigadier General George C. Wynkoop[130]
1st Pennsylvania: Colonel Samuel Yohe
2nd Pennsylvania: Colonel Frederick S. Stumbaugh
3rd Pennsylvania: Colonel Francis P. Minier
5th Brigade: Brigadier General James S. Negley[131]
14th Pennsylvania: Colonel John W. Johnston
15th Pennsylvania: Colonel Richard A. Oakford
24th Pennsylvania: Colonel Joshua T. Owen
6th Brigade: Colonel John J. Abercrombie[132]

---

[124] Samuel P. Bates, *History of Pennsylvania Volunteers, 1861-65 Vol. 1,* (Harrisburg: B. Singerly, 1869), 58
[125] Welcher, *The Union Army Vol. 1,* 74
[126] Bates, *Pennsylvania Volunteers Vol. 1,* 68
[127] Roger D. Hunt, *Colonels in Blue: Pennsylvania, New Jersey, Maryland, Delaware, and the District of Columbia,* (Stackpole, 2007), 64
[128] "On the 17th of June, Colonel Miles, with his detachments of the Second, Third, and Eighth regiments of U. S. infantry, was ordered to Washington. He accordingly turned over the command of the balance of the Brigade to Colonel Longenecker, the ranking officer, and ordered him to return to Williamsport with the three volunteer regiments, and report in person to the commanding General of the Division, Major General Cadwalader." Bates, *Pennsylvania Volunteers, Vol. 1,* 87
[129] Bates, *Pennsylvania Volunteers, Vol. 1,* 89 notes that Hangen was the senior officer behind Longenecker so it can be inferred that he assumed command of the regiment.
[130] Bates, *Pennsylvania Volunteers, Vol. 1,* 14.
[131] Bates, *Pennsylvania Volunteers, Vol. 1,* 214
[132] Bates, *Pennsylvania Volunteers, Vol. 1,* 107

11th Pennsylvania: Colonel Phaon Jarrett
1st Wisconsin: Colonel John C. Starkweather
4th Connecticut: Colonel Levi Woodhouse
2nd Massachusetts: Colonel George H. Gordon[133]

3rd Division: Major General Charles W. Sanford[134]
7th Brigade: Colonel Charles P. Stone[135]
1st New Hampshire: Colonel Mason Tappan
83rd New York (9th New York State Militia): Colonel John W. Stiles
17th Pennsylvania: Colonel Francis E. Patterson
25th Pennsylvania: Colonel Henry L. Cake
8th Brigade: Colonel Daniel Butterfield
5th New York: Colonel Christian Schwarzwaelder[136]
12th New York: Colonel Daniel Butterfield[137]
19th New York: Colonel John S. Clarke[138]
28th New York: Colonel Dudley Donnelly[139]

Unattached Infantry[140]
11th Indiana: Colonel Lewis Wallace[141]
3rd Wisconsin: Colonel Charles S. Hamilton[142]
4th Wisconsin: Colonel Halbert E. Paine[143]

Artillery[144]
A, 1st Rhode Island Artillery: Captain William H. Reynolds
F, 4th United States Artillery: Captain Delevan D. Perkins

Confederate Forces[145]
Army of the Potomac
Brigadier General Pierre G. T. Beauregard

---

[133] Joined Brigade July 14, 1861, Welcher, *The Union Army, Vol. 1*, 77
[134] Organized July 10, 1861, Welcher, *The Union Army, Vol. 1*, 76
[135] Dyer, *Compendium, Vol. 1*, 270
[136] Phisterer, *New York*, 532
[137] Phisterer, *New York*, 577
[138] Phisterer, *New York*, 1956; Later Designated 3rd New York Light Artillery
[139] Phisterer, *New York*, 2053
[140] Welcher, *The Union Army, Vol. 1*, 77
[141] Arrived July 19, Welcher, *The Union Army, Vol. 1*, 77
[142] Arrived July 20, Welcher, *The Union Army, Vol. 1*, 77
[143] Arrived July 20, Welcher, *The Union Army, Vol. 1*, 77
[144] Welcher, *The Union Army, Vol. 1*, 74
[145] *B&L Vol. 1*, 195

1st Brigade: Brigadier General Milledge L. Bonham
8th Louisiana: Colonel Henry B. Kelly[146]
1st South Carolina: Colonel Maxcy Gregg[147]
2nd South Carolina: Colonel Joseph B. Kershaw
3rd South Carolina: Colonel James H. Williams
7th South Carolina: Colonel Thomas G. Bacon
8th South Carolina: Colonel Ellerbee B. C. Cash
11th North Carolina: Colonel William W. Kirkland

2nd Brigade: Brigadier General Richard S. Ewell
5th Alabama: Colonel Robert E. Rodes
6th Alabama: Colonel John J. Seibels
6th Louisiana: Colonel Isaac G. Seymour

3rd Brigade: Brigadier General David R. Jones
17th Mississippi: Colonel Winfield S. Featherston
18th Mississippi: Colonel Erasmus R. Burt[148]
5th South Carolina: Colonel Micah Jenkins

4th Brigade: Colonel George H. Terrett
    Brigadier General James Longstreet[149]
5th North Carolina: Colonel Duncan K. McRae
    Lieutenant Colonel Joseph P. Jones[150]
1st Virginia: Colonel Patrick T. Moore (w)
    Major Frederick G. Skinner[151]
11th Virginia: Colonel Samuel Garland Jr.
17th Virginia: Colonel Montgomery D. Corse

5th Brigade: Colonel Philip St. George Cocke
8th Virginia: Colonel Eppa Hunton
18th Virginia: Colonel Robert E. Withers
19th Virginia: Lieutenant Colonel John B. Strange
28th Virginia: Colonel Robert T. Preston

---

[146] *OR, Series I, Vol. II,* 450

[147] *OR, Series I, Vol. II,* 943

[148] Bruce S. Allardice, *Confederate Colonels: A Biographical Register* (Columbia Mo.: University of Missouri Press, 2008), 84; Sifakis, *Confederate: Mississippi*, 102

[149] OR, Series I, Vol. II, 944; William C. Davis, *Battle at Bull Run* (New York: Doubleday, 1977), 59. Terrett commanded brigade for 2 weeks before Longstreet assumed command

[150] Jones commanded regiment as McRae was ill see *OR, Series I, Vol. II,* 543

[151] Moore wounded in the head July 18 at Blackburn's Ford and turned command over to Skinner, see *OR, Series I, Vol. II,* 445; Jack D. Welsh, *Medical Histories of Confederate Generals*, (Kent State University Press, 1999), 158

49th Virginia (3 companies): Colonel William Smith

6th Brigade: Colonel Jubal A. Early
7th Louisiana: Colonel Harry T. Hays
13th Mississippi: Colonel William Barksdale
7th Virginia: Colonel James L. Kemper
24th Virginia: Lieutenant Colonel Peter Hairston[152]

Evans' Command: Colonel Nathan G. Evans
1st Louisiana Battalion: Major Chatham Roberdeau Wheat (w)
          Captain Robert A. Harris[153]
4th South Carolina: Colonel John B. E. Sloan
Section, Virginia (Latham) Artillery: Lieutenant George S. Davidson[154]
2nd Virginia Cavalry (Company A [Clay Dragoons]): Captain William R. Terry[155]
2nd Virginia Cavalry (Company I [Campbell Rangers]): Captain John D. Alexander[156]

Reserve Brigade: Brigadier General Theophilus H. Holmes
1st Arkansas: Colonel James F. Fagan[157]
2nd Tennessee: Colonel William B. Bate[158]

Unattached Infantry:
Hampton (South Carolina) Legion: Colonel Wade Hampton (w)
          Captain James Conner[159]

Artillery: Colonel Samuel Jones[160]
Louisiana (Washington Artillery) Artillery Battalion: Major James B. Walton[161]
1st Company: Captain Harry M. Isaacson
2nd Company: Lieutenant Thomas L. Rosser
3rd Company: Captain Merritt B. Miller
4th Company: Captain Benjamin F. Eshelman

---

[152] Attached to Longstreet's brigade during the battle of 1st Manassas, see *OR, Series I, Vol. II*, 543, 555
[153] Wheat wounded July 21, "shot through both lungs" *OR, Series I, Vol. II*, 499-500, 558
[154] *OR, Series I, Vol. II,* 553
[155] Wallace, *Virginia*, 41
[156] Wallace, *Virginia*, 42
[157] Sifakis, *Confederate: Florida and Arkansas*, 67-68; Ezra J. Warner, *Generals in Gray*, (Baton Rouge: Louisiana State University Press, 1987), 85-86
[158] Warner, *Generals in Gray*, 19-20
[159] *OR, Series I, Vol. II, 567* For Hampton's wounding July 21 and Conner's succession
[160] *OR, Series I, Vol. II*, 446
[161] *OR, Series I, Vol. II*, 465-67; Sibley, *Confederate Artillery Organizations*, 310-11

Virginia (Alexandria Artillery) Battery: Captain Delaware Kemper
Virginia (Latham) Battery: Captain Henry Grey Latham
Virginia (Loudoun Artillery) Battery: Captain Arthur L. Rogers
Virginia (1st Company, Richmond Howitzers) Battery: Captain James C. Shields
Virginia (Purcell Artillery) Battery: Captain Reuben Lindsay Walker[162]

Cavalry
30th Virginia Cavalry: Colonel Richard C. W. Radford
Cavalry Battalion: Lieutenant Colonel Walter H. Jenifer[163]
Independent Cavalry Companies: Major Julian Harrison[164]
4th Virginia Cavalry (Company A [Prince William Cavalry]): Captain William W. Thornton
4th Virginia Cavalry (Company B [Chesterfield Light Dragoons]): Captain William B. Ball
4th Virginia Cavalry (Company D [Little Fork Rangers]): Captain Robert E. Utterback
4th Virginia Cavalry (Company E [Powhatan Troop]): Captain John F. Lay
4th Virginia Cavalry (Company F [Goochland Light Dragoons]): Captain George F. Harrison
4th Virginia Cavalry (Company G [Hanover Light Dragoons]): Captain Williams C. Wickham
4th Virginia Cavalry (Company H [Black Horse Troop]): Captain William H.F. Payne
4th Virginia Cavalry (Company I [Governor's Mounted Guard]): Captain John G. Cabell

Army of the Shenandoah
General Joseph E. Johnston

1st Brigade: Brigadier General Thomas J. Jackson (w)[165]
2nd Virginia: Colonel James W. Allen (w)
        Lieutenant Colonel Francis Lackland[166]
4th Virginia: Colonel James F. Preston (w)
        Lieutenant Colonel Lewis T. Moore[167]
5th Virginia: Colonel Kenton Harper
27th Virginia: Lieutenant Colonel John Echols
33rd Virginia: Colonel Arthur C. Cummings
Virginia (1st Rockbridge Artillery) Battery: Captain William N. Pendleton[168]

2nd Brigade: Colonel Francis S. Bartow (k)

---

[162] Wise, *Long Arm Vol. II*; OR, Series I, Vol. II, 491
[163] *OR, Series I, Vol. II*, 537
[164] 4th Virginia Cavalry not officially organized until September 19, 1861. Companies Served independently. Wallace, *Virginia*, 43-44
[165] Jackson did not leave the field. *OR, Series I, Vol. II*, 478
[166] See Dennis E. Frye, *2nd Virginia Infantry* (Lynchburg, Va., 1982), 15 for Allen, who was temporarily blinded, by fragments from an artillery shell striking a tree, and Lackland's succession
[167] Allardice, *Confederate Colonels,* 313
[168] Wise, *Long Arm Vol. II*, 989

                Colonel Lucius J. Gartrell[169]
7th Georgia: Colonel Lucius J. Gartrell
8th Georgia: Lieutenant Colonel William M. Gardner (w)
                Major Thomas L. Cooper[170]
9th Georgia: Colonel Edwin R. Goulding[171]
11th Georgia: Colonel George T. Anderson[172]
1st Kentucky Battalion: Lieutenant Colonel Blanton Duncan[173]
Kentucky Infantry Battalion: Lieutenant Colonel Thomas H. Taylor[174]
Virginia (Wise Artillery) Battery: Captain Ephraim G. Alburtis
                Lieutenant John Pelham[175]

<u>3rd Brigade</u>: Brigadier General Barnard E. Bee (k)
                Major William H. C. Whiting[176]
4th Alabama: Colonel Egbert J. Jones (mw)
                Colonel States Rights Gist[177]
2nd Mississippi: Colonel William C. Falkner
11th Mississippi: Colonel William H. Moore[178]
6th North Carolina: Colonel Charles F. Fisher (k)
                Lieutenant Colonel Charles E. Lightfoot (w)
              Major Robert F. Webb[179]

---

[169] Bartow shot through the heart rallying his troops on July 21, see Bruce S. Allardice, *More Generals in Gray*, (Louisiana State University Press, 1995), 31; Steven M. Smith and Patrick Hook, *The Stonewall Brigade in the Civil War* (Minneapolis, Zenith Press, 2008), 21 claims that Gartrell assumed brigade command upon Bartow's death; however I have been unable to find any supporting evidence. Only 7th and 8th Georgia engaged at Manassas see, *OR, Series I, Vol. II,* 569; see Davis, *Bull Run*, 83 for 9th Georgia. See *OR, Series I, Vol. II,* 470, for the Kentucky Battalions

[170] Severely wounded in the leg July 21, Welsh, *Medical Histories of Confederate* Generals, 75; *OR, Series I, Vol. II,* 477; Lillian Henderson, ed., *Roster of the Confederate soldiers of Georgia, 1861-1865 Volume 1*, (Longino & Porter, 1960), 955

[171] *OR, Series IV, Vol. 1,* 789; Allardice, *Confederate Colonels*, 170

[172] *OR, Series IV, Vol. I,* 789; For the 11th Georgia, See Joseph E. Johnston, *Narrative of Military Operations Directed During the Late War Between the States*, (New York: D. Appelton and Company, 1874), 33

[173] Sifakis, *Confederate: Kentucky, Maryland, Missouri, The Confederate Units, and the Indian Units*, 31

[174] Sifakis, *Confederate: Kentucky, Maryland, Missouri, The Confederate Units, and the Indian Units*, 49

[175] Alburtis was ill and Pelham commanded in his place see Jerry H. Maxwell, *The Perfect Lion, The Life and Death of Confederate Artillerist John Pelham*, (Tuscaloosa: University of Alabama Press, 2011), 49; Wise, *Long Arm Vol. 2*, 987

[176] Eight companies of the 11th Mississippi and 1st Tennessee not engaged at Manassas, see *OR, Series I, Vol. II*, 569. See *OR Series I, Vol. II,* 470 for brigade organization. Bee mortally wounded by a bullet in the stomach on July 21 and died the following day, Smith, *The Gallant Dead*, 7, 8. for Whiting

[177] Jones mortally wounded July 21, shot through both hips, died September 21, 1861, Allardice, *Confederate Colonels,* 218. See Johnston, *Narrative*, 48 for Gist

[178] The 2 companies engaged at Manassas were commanded by Lt Col Philip F. Liddell *B&L Vol. 1,* 195; Sifakis, *Confederate: Mississippi*, 90-91

1st Tennessee Provisional Army: Colonel Peter Turney[180]
Virginia (Staunton Artillery) Battery: Captain John D. Imboden[181]

<u>4th Brigade</u>: Colonel Arnold Elzey
        Brigadier General Edmund Kirby Smith (w)
        Colonel Arnold Elzey[182]
1st Maryland: Lieutenant Colonel George H. Steuart[183]
3rd Tennessee Provisional Army: Colonel John C. Vaughn[184]
10th Virginia: Colonel Simeon B. Gibbons
13th Virginia: Colonel Ambrose Powell Hill[185]
Virginia (Newtown Artillery) Battery: Captain George A. Groves
                      Lieutenant Robert F. Beckham[186]

<u>5th Brigade</u>: Brigadier General Edmund Kirby Smith
        Colonel John H. Forney[187]
8th Alabama: Colonel John A. Winston[188]
9th Alabama: Colonel Cadmus M. Wilcox[189]
10th Alabama: Colonel John H. Forney
        Lieutenant Colonel James B. Martin[190]
11th Alabama: Colonel Sydenham Moore[191]
19th Mississippi: Colonel Christopher H. Mott[192]
38th Virginia: Colonel Edward C. Edmonds[193]

---

[179] Fisher killed July 21 by a bullet to the head. See, Richard W. Iobst, *The Bloody Sixth: The Sixth North Carolina Regiment Confederate States of America*, (Raleigh: North Carolina Confederate Centennial Commission, 1965), 23-24, for Fisher, Lightfoot, and Webb
[180] Sifakis, *Confederate: Tennessee*, 88-89
[181] Wise, *Long Arm Vol. 2*, 987
[182] As his brigade had not arrived on the battlefield, Smith assumed command of Elsey's brigade as senior officer but relinquished command back to Elzey upon being wounded July 21 in the left breast. Davis, *Bull Run*, 29, 38; Esmerelda Boyle, *Biographical Sketches of Distinguished Marylanders*, (Baltimore: Kelly, Piet, & Company, 1877), 314 claims that "General Smith was in command of a division formed by his own and Elsey's Brigade, but his own Brigade having not come up, he had really only Elsey's under his command."
[183] Sifakis, *Confederate: Kentucky, Maryland, Missouri, The Confederate Units, and the Indian Units*, 61-62
[184] Sifakis, *Confederate: Tennessee*, 94-95
[185] Sifakis, *Confederate: Virginia*, 185-86
[186] Evans ed, *CMH Vol. 3*, 97.; Sibley, *Confederate Artillery Organizations*, 101
[187] See, Johnston, *Narrative*, 33 for composition of Smith's Brigade; not engaged at Manassas save for Stanard's Battery; Boyle, *Biographical Sketches*, 314; Evans ed, *CMH Vol. 3*, 83. Forney commanded the Brigade in Smith's absence, *OR Series I, Vol. LI Part II*, 188-89
[188] Allardice, *Confederate Colonels*, 402
[189] See Willis Brewer, *Alabama, Her History, Resources, War Record, and Public Men: From 1540 to 1872*, (Montgomery: Barrett & Brown Steam Printers and Book Binders, 1872), 603 for Wilcox
[190] Brewer, *Alabama*, 605 for Forney and Martin
[191] Brewer, *Alabama*, 607 for Moore
[192] See *OR Series I, Vol. LI,* 189 for Mott

Virginia (Thomas Artillery) Battery: Captain Philip B. Stanard[194]

<u>Cavalry</u>
1st Virginia Cavalry: Colonel James E. B. Stuart

---

[193] Ibid for Edmonds
[194] Wise, *Long Arm Vol. 2*, 990

Wilson's Creek (Springfield or Oak Hills), Missouri[195]
August 10, 1861

Union Forces
Brigadier General Nathaniel Lyon (k)
Major Samuel D. Sturgis[196]

Chief of Artillery
Major Franz Backof

<u>1st Brigade</u>: Major Samuel D. Sturgis
Regular Battalion (Companies B, C, &D 1st Infantry &Wood's Company Rifle Recruits):
    Captain John B. Plummer (w)
    Captain Arch Houston[197]
2nd Missouri (Battalion): Major Peter J. Osterhaus
1st United States Cavalry (Company B): Lieutenant Charles W. Canfield
F, 2nd United States Artillery: Captain James Totten

<u>2nd Brigade</u>: Lieutenant Colonel George L. Andrews (w)[198]
Regular Battalion (Companies B&E, 2nd Infantry, Lothrop's Company General Service Recruits,
    & Morine's Company Rifle Recruits): Captain Frederick Steele
1st Missouri: Lieutenant Colonel George L. Andrews
Improvised Artillery Battery: Lieutenant John V. Dubois

<u>3rd Brigade</u>: Colonel George W. Deitzler (w)[199]
1st Iowa: Colonel John F. Bates
    Lieutenant Colonel William H. Merritt[200]
1st Kansas: Major John A. Halderman
2nd Kansas: Colonel Robert B. Mitchell (w)
    Lieutenant Colonel Charles W. Blair[201]
Home Guard Cavalry Battalion: Major Clark Wright

---

[195] *B&L Vol. 1*, 306; Maj. George E. Knapp U.S. Army Retired, *The Wilson's Creek Staff Ride and Battlefield Tour*, (Combat Studies Institute U.S. Army Command and General Staff College: Fort Leavenworth Kansas, 1993), 85-87
[196] Lyon wounded in head and leg, killed shortly after by a bullet to the chest. Smith, *The Gallant Dead*, 10-11; Holcombe & Adams, *An Account of the Battle of Wilson's Creek*, (Springfield Mo:Dow & Adams Publishers, 1883), 35-36. Sturgis was the senior officer on the field at the time of Lyon's death and assumed command *OR Series I, Vol. III, 62*
[197] See William Garrett Piston & Richard W. Hatcher III, *Wilson's Creek: The Second Battle of the Civil War and the Men Who Fought It*, (University of North Carolina Press, 2000), 219 for Plummer's wounding and Houston's succession
[198] Holcombe & Adams, *Wilson's Creek*, 86
[199] Wounded in the right leg, Welsh, *Medical Histories of Union Generals*, 94
[200] *OR Series I, Vol. III*, 81. Bates was ill and Merritt command the regiment at the battle.
[201] Holcombe & Adams, *Wilson's Creek*, 89 for Mitchell and Blair

Missouri Pioneers: Captain John D. Voerster

Missouri Volunteers 2nd Brigade: Colonel Franz Sigel
3rd Missouri: Lieutenant Colonel Anselm Albert
5th Missouri: Colonel Charles E. Salomon
1st United States Cavalry (Company I): Captain Eugene A. Carr
2nd United States Dragoons (Company C): Lieutenant Charles E. Farrend
Missouri Artillery Battery: Lieutenant Gustavus A. Schaefer & Lieutenant Edward Schutzenberg

Confederate Forces

McCulloch's Command
Brigadier General Benjamin McCulloch

Arkansas Brigade: Brigadier General Nicholas B. Pearce
1st Arkansas Cavalry: Colonel DeRossy Carroll
Arkansas Cavalry Company: Captain Charles A. Carroll
3rd Arkansas: Colonel John R. Gratiot
4th Arkansas: Colonel James D. Walker[202]
5th Arkansas: Colonel Thomas P. Dockery
Arkansas (Woodruff's) Battery: Captain William E. Woodruff Jr.[203]
Arkansas (Reid's [Fort Smith Battery]) Battery: Captain John G. Reid[204]

Brigade: Brigadier General Benjamin McCulloch
3rd Louisiana: Colonel Louis Hebert
1st Arkansas Mounted Rifles: Colonel Thomas J. Churchill
2nd Arkansas Mounted Rifles: Colonel James M. McIntosh
                              Lieutenant Colonel Benjamin T. Embry[205]
3rd Arkansas Battalion: Lieutenant Colonel Dandridge McRae[206]
South Kansas-Texas Mounted Regiment: Colonel Elkanah Greer

Missouri State Guard
Major. General Sterling Price

3rd Division: Brigadier General John B. Clark Sr. (w)[207]

---

[202] Sifakis, *Confederate: Florida and Arkansas*, 79
[203] Sibley, *Confederate Artillery Organizations*, 319
[204] Sibley, *Confederate Artillery Organizations*, 220
[205] McIntosh served as McCulloch's adjutant throughout the battle leaving Embry in command of the regiment. Piston & Hatcher, *Wilson's Creek*, 217
[206] Sifakis, *Confederate: Florida and Arkansas*, 73

1st Missouri State Guard: Colonel John Q. Burbridge (w)
    Major John B. Clark Jr.[208]
1st Missouri State Guard Cavalry Battalion: Major James P. Major[209]

4th Division: Brigadier General William Y. Slack (w)
    Colonel Benjamin A. Rives[210]
1st Missouri State Guard: Colonel John T. Hughes[211]
1st Missouri State Guard Battalion: Major John C. C. Thornton[212]
1st Missouri State Guard Cavalry: Colonel Benjamin A. Rives
    Lieutenant Colonel Andrew J. Austin (k)
    Lieutenant Colonel Louis C. Bohannon[213]

6th Division: Brigadier General Mosby Monroe Parsons
1st Missouri State Guard: Colonel Joseph Kelly (w)[214]
1st Missouri State Guard Cavalry: Colonel William B. Brown[215]
1st Missouri State Guard Light Artillery Battery: Captain Henry C. Guibor
    Lieutenant William P. Barlow
    Captain Henry C. Guibor[216]

7th Division: Brigadier General John H. McBride
1st Missouri State Guard: Colonel Edmund T. Wingo[217]
2nd Missouri State Guard: Colonel John A. Foster (mw)
    Lieutenant Colonel John H. Forbes[218]

---

[207] See Holcombe & Adams, *Wilson's Creek*, 65
[208] Peterson et al, *Price's Lieutenants*, 164. See Eathan Allen Pinnell, *Serving with Honor: The Diary of Captain Eathan Allen Pinnell, Eighth Missouri Infantry (Confederate)*, (NP:ND), 378 for Burbridge, who was "severely wounded in the head," and for Clark's succession
[209] Peterson et al, *Price's Lieutenants*, 163
[210] See, Smith, *The Gallant Dead*, 24, for Slack who was severely wounded in the hip; Peterson et al, *Price's Lieutenants*, 194
[211] Peterson et al, *Price's Lieutenants*, 203
[212] Peterson et al, *Price's Lieutenants*, 229-30. From 5th Division
[213] See, Peterson et al, *Price's Lieutenants*, 196 for Austin and Bohannon
[214] Peterson et al, *Price's Lieutenants*, 273. See, Holcombe & Adams, *Wilson's Creek*, 65, for Kelly who was wounded in the hand
[215] Commander listed in reports as Ben Brown, who was killed at Wilson's Creek, however, according to Peterson et al, *Price's Lieutenants*, 31, 194, 258 Ben Brown was inspector general of the 4th Division, and the regiment was commanded by Col William B. Brown
[216] Guibor temporarily separated from his command, Barlow commanded in the interim. Piston & Hatcher, *Wilson's Creek*; Peterson et al, *Price's Lieutenants*, 285
[217] Peterson et al, *Price's Lieutenants*, 301
[218] Foster wounded in the leg, subsequently died of gangrene see Vicky Layton Cobb, *Ozark Pioneers*, (Arcadia Publishing, 2001), 68; Peterson et al, *Price's Lieutenants*, 303

1st Missouri State Guard Cavalry Battalion (Company E): Captain Leonidas St. Clair Campbell[219]

8th Division: Brigadier General James S. Rains
Infantry Brigade: Colonel Richard H. Weightman (mw)
    Colonel John R. Graves[220]
1st Missouri State Guard: Lieutenant Colonel Thomas H. Rosser
2nd Missouri State Guard: Colonel John R. Graves
    Major Ezra J. Brashear
3rd Missouri State Guard: Colonel Edgar V.R. Hurst
4th Missouri State Guard Battalion: Major Thomas H. Murray
5th Missouri State Guard: Colonel James J. Clarkson
Cavalry Brigade: Colonel James Cawthorn (mw)
    Lieutenant Colonel John W. Martin
    Colonel Jeremiah C. Cravens[221]
1st Missouri State Guard Cavalry (elements): Lieutenant Colonel John W. Martin[222]
2nd Missouri State Guard Cavalry: Lieutenant Colonel James C. McCown[223]
3rd Missouri State Guard Cavalry: Colonel Robert L.Y. Peyton[224]
4th Missouri State Guard Cavalry: Lieutenant Colonel Benjamin F. Walker[225]
5th Missouri State Guard Cavalry: Colonel Jeremiah C. Cravens
    Lieutenant Colonel Thomas H. Slover[226]
6th Missouri State Guard Cavalry: Lieutenant Colonel John W. Payne[227]
7th Missouri State Guard Cavalry: Colonel DeWitt C. Hunter[228]
Artillery
1st (Price's Rifles) Missouri State Guard Light Artillery Battery: Captain Hiram M. Bledsoe[229]

---

[219] Peterson et al, *Price's Lieutenants*, 299-300
[220] Weightman hit in 3 places and killed. See *OR Series I, Vol. III,* 101
[221] Cawthorn was wounded in the foot, which was subsequently amputated. Cawthorn died Aug 18. See Louis S. Gerties, *The Civil War in Missouri: A Military History*, (University of Missouri Press, 2012), 216; See, Peterson et al, *Price's Lieutenants*, 356 for Martin and Cravens
[222] Peterson et al, *Price's Lieutenants*, 357-61
[223] Peterson et al, *Price's Lieutenants*, 361-67
[224] Peterson et al, *Price's Lieutenants*, 368-72
[225] Peterson et al, *Price's Lieutenants*, 372-76
[226] Peterson et al, *Price's Lieutenants*, 376-80
[227] Peterson et al, *Price's Lieutenants*, 380-85
[228] Peterson et al, *Price's Lieutenants*, 385-89
[229] Peterson et al, *Price's Lieutenants*, 410

Kessler's Cross-Lanes (Cross-Lanes, Summerville), West Virginia
August 26, 1861

Union Forces[230]

7th Ohio: Colonel Erastus B. Tyler[231]

Confederate Forces[232]
Army of the Kanawha
Brigadier General John B. Floyd

22nd Virginia: Colonel Christopher Q. Tompkins[233]
36th Virginia: Lieutenant Colonel John McCausland[234]
45th Virginia: Colonel Henry Heth[235]
50th Virginia: Colonel Alexander W. Reynolds[236]
51st Virginia: Colonel Gabriel C. Wharton[237]
59th Virginia (Companies A & B): Captain Obadiah Jennings Wise[238]

Cavalry
Border Guards: Captain Albert J. Beckett
Border Rangers (Company E, 8th Virginia Cavalry): Captain James M. Corns
Nelson Rangers (Company B, 8th Virginia Cavalry): Captain Thomas P. Fitzpatrick
Smyth Dragoons (Company A, 8th Virginia Cavalry): Captain John H. Thompson

Artillery
Virginia (Gauley Artillery) Battery: Captain Stephen A. Adams[239]
Virginia (Goochland Artillery) Battery: Captain John H. Guy[240]
Virginia (Kanawha Artillery) Battery: Lieutenant Thomas E. Jackson[241]

---

[230] Phisterer, *Statistical Record*, 86
[231] *OR Series I, Vol. V*, 118
[232] Lowry, *September Blood*, 31-42
[233] Wallace, *Virginia*, 104-05 Sifakis, *Confederate: Virginia*, 200-01.
[234] Lowry, *Scary Creek*, 17; Wallace, *Virginia*, 118-19; Sifakis, *Confederate: Virginia*, 223-24
[235] Sifakis, *Confederate: Virginia*, 234-35
[236] Sifakis, *Confederate: Virginia*, 240-41
[237] Sifakis, *Confederate: Virginia*, 242-43
[238] Wallace, *Virginia*, 136-37, 52
[239] Sibley, *Confederate Artillery Organizations*, 11
[240] *OR Series I, Vol. V, 147*; Wise, *Long Arm Vol. 2*, 988
[241] Sibley, *Confederate Artillery Organizations*, 114-15

Hatteras Expedition, North Carolina
August 26-29, 1861

Union Forces[242]
Major. General Benjamin F. Butler

9th New York: Colonel Rush C. Hawkins
20th New York: Colonel Max Weber
United States Coast Guard Company: Captain Richard Nixon
H, 2nd United States Artillery: Lieutenant Frank H. Larned

Union Naval Forces[243]
Flag Officer Silas H. Stringham

U.S.S. Cumberland: Captain John Marston
U.S.S. Minnesota: Captain Gershom J. Van Brunt[244]
U.S.S. Monticello: Commander. John P. Gillis
U.S.S. Pawnee: Commander. Samuel C. Rowan
U.S.S. Susquehanna: Captain John S. Chauncey
U.S.S. Wabash: Captain Samuel Mercer

<u>Infantry Transports</u>
U.S.S. Adelaide: Commander. Henry S. Stellwagen
U.S.S. George Peabody: Lieutenant Reigart B. Lowry[245]
U.S.S. Fanny: Lieutenant Pierce Crosby

Confederate Forces[246]

Fort Hatteras Garrison (1st North Carolina Artillery, Company F): Major William S. G. Andrews[247]
7th North Carolina: Colonel William Martin
Unspecified Naval Force: Flag Officer Samuel Barron

---

[242] *OR Series I, Vol. IV,* 581
[243] *Official records of the Union and Confederate Navies in the War of the Rebellion Series I, Vol. 6,* (Government Printing Office: Washington D.C., 1897), 120-21. Hereafter cited as *ORN*
[244] Dictionary of American Naval Fighting Ships, "Minnesota," *Naval History and Heritage Command.* Accessed February 26, 2014. http://www.history.navy.mil/research/histories/ship-histories/danfs.html
[245] Officers of the Continental and U.S. Navy and Marine Corps 1775-1900, "Navy Officers 1798-1900, L," *Naval History and Heritage Command.* Accessed February 26, 2014. http://www.history.navy.mil/browse-by-topic/organization-and-administration/historical-leadership/navy-and-marine-corps-officers-1775-1900.html
[246] *OR Series I, Vol. IV,* 586-87
[247] Sifakis, *Confederate: North Carolina,* 11-12

Dry Wood Creek (Fort Scott), Missouri
September 2, 1861

Union Forces[248]
Brigadier General James H. Lane

3rd Kansas: Colonel James Montgomery
4th Kansas: Colonel William A. Weer
5th Kansas Cavalry: Colonel Hampton P. Johnson[249]
6th Kansas Cavalry: Colonel William R. Judson[250]
7th Kansas Cavalry: Colonel Charles R. Jennison
1st Kansas Light Artillery: Captain Thomas Bickerton[251]

Confederate Forces
Brigadier General James S. Rains & Brigadier General Alexander E. Steen[252]

3rd Division
1st Missouri State Guard: Lieutenant Colonel Edwin Price & Major. John B. Clark Jr.[253]
1st Missouri State Guard Battalion: Lieutenant Colonel Robert S. Bevier[254]
2nd Missouri State Guard Battalion: Lieutenant Colonel Middleton G. Singleton & Major Quinton L. Peacher[255]

4th Division
1st Missouri State Guard: Colonel John T. Hughes[256]
1st Missouri State Guard Cavalry: Lieutenant Colonel Louis C. Bohannon[257]

5th Division
1st Missouri State Guard Cavalry Battalion: Major John C. C. Thornton[258]

6th Division

---

[248] Welcher, *The Union Army, Vol. 2*, 70
[249] *The Union Army: A History of Military Affairs in the Loyal States 1861-65, Vol. 4*, (Federal Publishing Company: Madison Wis., 1908), 206. Hereafter referred to as *Union*
[250] *Union, Vol. 4*, 207
[251] *Union, Vol. 4*, 222
[252] Steen had overall command of the cavalry at this battle, see, Peterson et al, *Price's Lieutenants*, 217
[253] Peterson et al, *Price's Lieutenants*, 164-69
[254] Serving as mounted infantry, Peterson et al, *Price's Lieutenants*, 188
[255] Peterson et al, *Price's Lieutenants*, 188
[256] Peterson et al, *Price's Lieutenants*, 203-09
[257] Peterson et al, *Price's Lieutenants*, 196-201
[258] Peterson et al, *Price's Lieutenants*, 229-30

2nd Missouri State Guard: Colonel George K. Dills[259]
1st Missouri State Guard Light Artillery Battery: Captain Henry C. Guibor[260]

7th Division
2nd Missouri State Guard: Colonel Archibald A. MacFarlane[261]
1st Missouri State Guard Cavalry Battalion (Company E): Captain Leonidas St. Clair Campbell[262]

8th Division
1st Missouri State Guard: Colonel Thomas H. Rosser[263]
2nd Missouri State Guard: Colonel John R. Graves[264]
3rd Missouri State Guard: Colonel Edgar V.R. Hurst[265]
4th Missouri State Guard Battalion: Lieutenant Colonel Walter S. O'Kane[266]
5th Missouri State Guard: Colonel James J. Clarkson[267]
1st Missouri State Guard Cavalry (elements): Lieutenant Colonel John W. Martin[268]
2nd Missouri State Guard Cavalry: Colonel James C. McCown[269]
3rd Missouri State Guard Cavalry: Colonel Robert L.Y. Peyton[270]
4th Missouri State Guard Cavalry: Colonel Benjamin F. Walker[271]
5th Missouri State Guard Cavalry: Colonel Jeremiah C. Cravens[272]
6th Missouri State Guard Cavalry: Lieutenant Colonel John W. Payne[273]
7th Missouri State Guard Cavalry: Colonel DeWitt C. Hunter[274]
9th Missouri State Guard Cavalry Battalion: Lieutenant Colonel Thomas B. Cummings[275]
1st (Price's Rifles) Missouri State Guard Light Artillery Battery: Captain Hiram M. Bledsoe (w)
    Captain Emmett MacDonald[276]

---

[259] Peterson et al, *Price's Lieutenants*, 276-80
[260] Peterson et al, *Price's Lieutenants*, 285
[261] Peterson et al, *Price's Lieutenants*, 303-06
[262] Peterson et al, *Price's Lieutenants*, 299-300
[263] Peterson et al, *Price's Lieutenants*, 321-29
[264] Peterson et al, *Price's Lieutenants*, 329-36
[265] Peterson et al, *Price's Lieutenants*, 336-41
[266] Peterson et al, *Price's Lieutenants*, 342-47
[267] Peterson et al, *Price's Lieutenants*, 347-51
[268] Peterson et al, *Price's Lieutenants*, 357-61
[269] Peterson et al, *Price's Lieutenants*, 361-67
[270] Peterson et al, *Price's Lieutenants*, 368-72
[271] Peterson et al, *Price's Lieutenants*, 372-76
[272] Peterson et al, *Price's Lieutenants*, 376-80
[273] Peterson et al, *Price's Lieutenants*, 380-85
[274] Peterson et al, *Price's Lieutenants*, 385-89
[275] Peterson et al, *Price's Lieutenants*, 390-92
[276] Peterson et al, *Price's Lieutenants*, 410; Severely wounded in the groin, *History of Lafayette County Missouri* (Missouri Historical Company: St. Louis, 1881), 340

Carnifex Ferry, West Virginia
September 10, 1861

Union Forces[277]
Brigadier General William S. Rosecrans

1st Brigade[278]: Brigadier General Henry W. Benham
10th Ohio: Colonel William H. Lytle (w)
      Lieutenant Colonel Hermann J. Korff[279]
12th Ohio: Colonel John W. Lowe (k)
      Lieutenant Colonel Carr B. White[280]
13th Ohio: Colonel William Sooy Smith[281]
1st West Virginia Cavalry (2 companies): Captain William A. West & Captain George L. Gilmore
1st Ohio Independent Battery: Captain James R. McMullin[282]
2 6 lb. rifled guns: Captain George Schneider[283]

2nd Brigade: Colonel Robert L. McCook[284]
9th Ohio: Lieutenant Colonel Charles Sondershoff[285]
28th Ohio: Colonel Augustus Moor[286]
47th Ohio: Colonel Frederick Poschner[287]
Chicago Dragoons: Captain Frederick Schambeck[288]

3rd Brigade: Colonel Eliakim Parker Scammon[289]
23rd Ohio: Lieutenant Colonel Stanley Matthews
30th Ohio: Colonel Hugh B. Ewing[290]
I, 4th United States Artillery: Captain Oscar A. Mack

Confederate Forces[291]

---

[277] Dyer, *Compendium Vol. 1*, 335
[278] Lowry, *September Blood*, 47-53
[279] Lytle wounded in the leg, *OR Series I, Vol. V*, 136
[280] Lowe "instantly killed by a discharge of canister" *OR Series I, Vol. V*, 134, 138 for White
[281] *OR Series I, Vol. V*, 130
[282] *OR Series I, Vol. V*, 130
[283] Organized from Company E, 13th Ohio, Lowry, *September Blood*, 53
[284] Lowry, *September Blood*, 54-57
[285] *OR Series I, Vol. V,*, 142
[286] *OR Series I, Vol. V*, 143
[287] *OR Series I, Vol. V*, 144
[288] *OR Series I, Vol. V*, 144
[289] Lowry, *September Blood*, 57-63
[290] *OR Series I, Vol. V*, 145

Army of the Kanawha
Brigadier General John B. Floyd

22nd Virginia: Colonel Christopher Q. Tompkins[292]
36th Virginia: Lieutenant Colonel John McCausland[293]
45th Virginia: Colonel Henry Heth[294]
50th Virginia: Colonel Alexander W. Reynolds[295]
51st Virginia: Colonel Gabriel C. Wharton[296]
59th Virginia (Companies A & B): Captain Obadiah Jennings Wise[297]

<u>Cavalry</u>
Border Guards: Captain Albert J. Beckett
Border Rangers (Company E, 8th Virginia Cavalry): Captain James M. Corns
Nelson Rangers (Company B, 8th Virginia Cavalry): Captain Thomas P. Fitzpatrick
Smyth Dragoons (Company A, 8th Virginia Cavalry): Captain John H. Thompson

<u>Artillery</u>
Virginia (Gauley Artillery) Battery: Captain Stephen A. Adams[298]
Virginia (Goochland Artillery) Battery: Captain John H. Guy[299]
Virginia (Kanawha Artillery) Battery: Lieutenant Thomas E. Jackson[300]

---

[291] *OR Series IV, Vol. I*, 630-31; Lowry, *September Blood*, 31-42
[292] Wallace, *Virginia*, 104-05 Sifakis, *Confederate: Virginia*, 200-01.
[293] Lowry, *Scary Creek*, 17; Wallace, *Virginia*, 118-19; Sifakis, *Confederate: Virginia*, 223-24
[294] Sifakis, *Confederate: Virginia*, 234-35
[295] Sifakis, *Confederate: Virginia*, 240-41
[296] Sifakis, *Confederate: Virginia*, 242-43
[297] Wallace, *Virginia*, 136-37, 52
[298] Sibley, *Confederate Artillery Organizations*, 11
[299] *OR Series I, Vol. V, 147*; Wise, *Long Arm Vol. 2*, 988
[300] Sibley, *Confederate Artillery Organizations*, 114-15

Cheat Mountain Campaign, West Virginia
September 10-17, 1861

Union Forces
Cheat Mountain District[301]
Brigadier General Joseph J. Reynolds

3rd Ohio: Colonel Isaac H. Morrow[302]
6th Ohio: Colonel William K. Bosley[303]
24th Ohio: Colonel Jacob Ammen[304]
25th Ohio: Colonel John A. Jones[305]
32nd Ohio: Colonel Thomas H. Ford[306]
7th Indiana: Colonel James Gavin[307]
9th Indiana: Colonel Robert H. Milroy[308]
13th Indiana: Colonel Jeremiah C. Sullivan[309]
14th Indiana: Colonel Nathan Kimball[310]
15th Indiana: Colonel George D. Wagner[311]
17th Indiana: Colonel Milo S. Haskell[312]
2nd West Virginia: Colonel John W. Moss[313]
3rd West Virginia: Colonel David T. Hewes[314]

Cavalry

1st Ohio Cavalry (Company A): Captain John H. Robinson[315]
1st Ohio Cavalry (Company C): Captain Nathan D. Menken[316]
Indiana Cavalry Company: Captain James R. Bracken[317]

Artillery

Rigby's Indiana Battery: Captain Silas F. Rigby[318]

---

[301] Dyer, *Compendium Vol. 1*, 335; Jack Zinn, *R.E. Lee's Cheat Mountain Campaign*, (McClain Print Co., 1974), 113
[302] *Ohio Vol. 1*, 39.
[303] *Ohio Vol. 1*, 107
[304] *Ohio, Vol. 3*, 139
[305] *Ohio, Vol. 3*, 167
[306] *Ohio, Vol. 3*, 471
[307] *Report of the Adjutant General of the State of Indiana Vol. 2 1861-1865*, (Indianapolis: W.B. Holloway State Printer, 1865), 40. Hereafter referred to as *Indiana*.
[308] *Union, Vol. 3*, 112
[309] *Union, Vol. 3*, 116
[310] *Union, Vol. 3*, 117
[311] *Union, Vol. 3*, 118
[312] *Union, Vol. 3*, 119
[313] *OR, Series I, Vol. V*, 185
[314] *Union Army, Vol. 2*. 300
[315] *Ohio, Vol. 11*, 5
[316] *Ohio, Vol. 11*, 12
[317] *Union, Vol. 3*, 128

A, 1st Michigan Artillery: Captain Cyrus O. Loomis[319]
12th Ohio Independent Battery: Captain Aaron C. Johnson[320]
G, 4th United States Artillery: Captain Albion P. Howe
A, 1st West Virginia Artillery: Captain Philip Daum[321]

Confederate Forces
Army of the Northwest[322]
Major General Robert E. Lee

Huntersville Division: Brigadier General William W. Loring
2nd Brigade: Brigadier General Samuel R. Anderson[323]
1st Tennessee: Colonel George Maney
7th Tennessee: Colonel Robert Hatton
14th Tennessee: Colonel William A. Forbes
Virginia (Hampden Artillery) Battery: Captain Lawrence S. Marye[324]
Cavalry Company: Lieutenant W. Alexander
3rd Brigade: Brigadier General Daniel S. Donelson[325]
8th Tennessee: Colonel Alfred S. Fulton
16th Tennessee: Colonel John H. Savage
14th Georgia: Colonel Arnoldus V. Brumby
Greenbrier Cavalry Company: Captain Robert B. Moorman[326]
4th Brigade: Colonel William Gilham
6th (16th) North Carolina: Colonel Stephen D. Lee[327]
21st Virginia: Lieutenant Colonel John M. Patton Jr.[328]
1st Battalion Confederate States Provisional Army: Major John D. Munford[329]
Georgia (Troup Artillery) Battery: Captain Henry H. Carlton[330]
6th Brigade: Colonel Jesse S. Burks

---

[318] *Union, Vol. 3*, 206
[319] *Union, Vol. 3*, 429
[320] *Union, Vol. 2*, 476
[321] *Union, Vol. 2*, 308
[322] *OR Series I, Vol. LI (Part II)*, 283-284; Evans ed, *CMH Vol. 3*, 152-57; Evans ed, *CMH Vol. 2 "West Virginia,"* 40
[323] Evans, *CMH, Vol.8*, 179
[324] Wise, *Long Arm, Vol. 2*, 985
[325] *OR Series I, Vol. V*, 938; Evans, *CMH, Vol. 8*, 179
[326] Wallace, *Virginia*, 79
[327] Sifakis, *Confederate: North Carolina*, 106-07
[328] John H. Worsham, *One of Jackson's Foot Cavalry*, (The Neale Publishing Company, 1912), 36 lists Patton as senior officer behind Col Gilham, so it can be inferred that he commanded the regiment while Gilham was in brigade command.
[329] Also known as the 1st Virginia Battalion see, Kenneth J. Radley, *Rebel Watchdog The Confederate States Army Provost Guard*, (LSU Press, 1989), 301
[330] Wise, *Long Arm, Vol. 2*, 987

42nd Virginia: Colonel Jesse S. Burks[331]
48th Virginia: Colonel John A. Campbell[332]
9th Virginia Cavalry (Companies G and H [Lee's Squadron]): Captain William H. F. Lee[333]

Monterey Division: Brigadier General Henry R. Jackson
1st Brigade: Colonel Albert Rust[334]
1st Georgia: Colonel James N. Ramsey[335]
12th Georgia: Colonel Edward Johnson[336]
3rd Arkansas: Lieutenant Colonel Seth M. Barton[337]
31st Virginia: Colonel William L. Jackson[338]
52nd Virginia: Colonel John F. Baldwin[339]
9th Virginia Battalion: Lieutenant Colonel George W. Hansbrough[340]
Virginia (Danville Artillery) Battery: Captain Lindsay M. Shumaker[341]
Cavalry Company: Captain George Jackson
5th Brigade: Colonel William B. Taliaferro[342]
23rd Virginia: Lieutenant Colonel Alexander G. Taliaferro[343]
25th Virginia: Colonel Jonathan M. Heck[344]
37th Virginia: Colonel Samuel V. Fulkerson[345]
44th Virginia: Colonel William C. Scott[346]
Virginia (8th Star Artillery) Battery: Captain William H. Rice[347]
Virginia (Lynchburg "Lee" Artillery) Battery: Captain Pierce B. Anderson[348]

---

[331] Wallace, *Virginia*, 123
[332] Wallace, *Virginia*, 129
[333] Wallace, *Virginia*, 76
[334] *OR Series I, Vol. V*, 233
[335] 1st Georgia was in Jackson's (Rust's) Brigade. George Winston Martin, *"I Will Give Them One More Shot": Ramsey's 1st Regiment Georgia Volunteers*, (Mercer University Press, 2005), 138
[336] *OR Series I, Vol. V*, 224
[337] See *OR Series I, Vol. V*, 233 for Barton
[338] Wallace, *Virginia*, 115
[339] Wallace, *Virginia*, 131-32
[340] Wallace, *Virginia*, 93-94
[341] Wise, *Long Arm Vol. 2*, 990
[342] *OR Series I, Vol. V*, 225
[343] Wallace, *Virginia*, 105-06
[344] *OR Series I, Vol. 5*, 187
[345] Wallace, *Virginia*, 119-20
[346] Wallace, *Virginia*, 124
[347] Wise, *Long Arm Vol. 2*, 990
[348] *OR Series I, Vol. V*, 463

Lewinsville, Virginia
September 11, 1861

Union Forces[349]
Brigadier General William F. Smith

19th Indiana (5 companies): Colonel Solomon Meredith
2nd Vermont (2 companies): Lieutenant Colonel George J. Stannard
3rd Vermont: Colonel Breed N. Hyde
79th New York: Colonel Isaac I. Stevens
1st United States Chasseurs (4 companies): Lieutenant Colonel Alexander Shaler
5th United States Cavalry (Company H): Lieutenant William McLean
40 man Cavalry Detachment: Captain O. O. G. Robinson
3rd New York Battery: Captain Thaddeus P. Mott
D, 5th United States Artillery: Captain Charles Griffin

Confederate Forces[350]
Colonel James E. B. Stuart

13th Virginia (Battalion): Major James B. Terrill
1st Virginia Cavalry (Company E [Valley Rangers]): Captain William Patrick[351]
Louisiana (2nd Company, Washington Artillery Battalion) Battery: Captain Thomas L. Rosser[352]

---

[349] Phisterer, *Statistical Record*, 87; *OR Series I, Vol. V*, 167-180
[350] *OR Series I, Vol. V*, 180-84
[351] Wallace, *Virginia*, 40
[352] Sibley, *Confederate Artillery Organizations*, 310

Siege of Lexington, Missouri
September 12-23, 1861

Union Forces[353]
Colonel James A. Mulligan (w&c)
Lieutenant Colonel Robert White (w&c)
Major. Frederick Becker (c) [354]

23rd Illinois: Colonel James A. Mulligan (w&c)[355]
13th Missouri: Colonel Everett Peabody (w&c)[356]
14th Missouri Home Guard: Lieutenant Colonel Robert White (w&c)[357]
Freedom Township Company: Major Frederick Becker (c)[358]
27th Missouri Mounted Infantry: Lieutenant Colonel Benjamin W. Grover (mw&c)[359]
U.S. Reserve Corps Infantry Battalion: Major Robert T. Van Horn (w&c)[360]
1st Illinois Cavalry (2 Battalions): Colonel Thomas A. Marshall (w&c)[361]
Lexington Home Guard Battery: Captain Charles M. Pirner (c)
Battery: Captain _ Adams[362] (c)

Confederate Forces
Missouri State Guard
Major. General Sterling Price

2nd Division: Brigadier General Thomas A. Harris[363]
1st Missouri State Guard: Colonel Edward C. McDonald[364]
1st Missouri State Guard Battalion: Major John M. Robinson[365]

---

[353] Entire garrison and officers captured see *OR, Series I, Vol. III,* 188
[354] Mulligan wounded in arm by grapeshot and leg by rifle ball. White assumed command and was subsequently "gravely wounded." Becker then assumed command and ordered the surrender See Larry Wood, *The Siege of Lexington Missouri: The Battle of the Hemp Bales* (The History Press, 2014), 104
[355] *History of Lafayette County Missouri*, 337
[356] *Lafayette County*, 338; Wood, *Lexington,* 104
[357] See, Wood, *Lexington,* 23, for White in Command; shot through the lungs, *Lafayette County,* 355
[358] *Lafayette County*, 338
[359] Grover was mortally wounded by a shell to the thigh; he died Oct 30, 1861. Budd Hannings, *Every Day of the Civil War: A Chronological History*, (McFarland, 2010), 83; *Missouri Historical Review, Volume 1, Issues 2-4,* (State Historical Society of Missouri, 1907), 136
[360] *Lafayette County*, 338; Wood, *Lexington,* 104
[361] *Lafayette County*, 337; Wounded in the chest. Wood, *Lexington,* 104
[362] *Lafayette County*, 338
[363] *OR, Series I, Vol. III,* 189-190
[364] Peterson et al, *Price's Lieutenants,* 140; Wood, *Lexington,* 88

2nd Missouri State Guard Battalion: Major James W. Robinson[366]
1st Missouri State Guard Cavalry: Colonel Martin E. Green[367]
2nd Missouri State Guard Cavalry: Lieutenant Colonel William C. Blanton[368]
3rd Missouri State Guard Cavalry: Lieutenant Colonel Theodore Brace[369]
4th Missouri State Guard Cavalry: Lieutenant Colonel Edward B. Hull Jr.[370]
1st Missouri State Guard Cavalry Battalion: Lieutenant Colonel George W. Riggins[371]
Palmyra Light Artillery Battery: Captain James W. Kneisley[372]

3rd Division: Colonel Congreve Jackson[373]
1st Missouri State Guard: Lieutenant Colonel Edwin Price & Major John B. Clark Jr.[374]
2nd Missouri State Guard: Lieutenant Colonel John R. White & Major Joseph Vaughan[375]
1st Missouri State Guard Battalion: Lieutenant Colonel Robert S. Bevier[376]
2nd Missouri State Guard Battalion: Lieutenant Colonel Middleton G. Singleton & Major Quinton L. Peacher[377]
Independent Companies: Colonel John A. Poindexter[378]
1st Missouri State Guard Cavalry Battalion: Lieutenant Colonel James P. Major & Major A. H. Chalmers[379]

4th Division: Colonel Benjamin A. Rives[380]
1st Missouri State Guard: Colonel John T. Hughes[381]
2nd Missouri State Guard: Colonel Thomas Jefferson Patton [382]
Missouri State Guard Battalion: Major Calvin B. Hansard[383]

---

[365] Peterson et al, *Price's Lieutenants*, 140-41
[366] Peterson et al, *Price's Lieutenants*, 142
[367] Peterson et al, *Price's Lieutenants*, 108-16
[368] Peterson et al, *Price's Lieutenants*, 116-18
[369] Peterson et al, *Price's Lieutenants*, 118-23
[370] Peterson et al, *Price's Lieutenants*, 124-29
[371] Peterson et al, *Price's Lieutenants*, 130-32
[372] Peterson et al, *Price's Lieutenants*, 148
[373] Jackson commanded the division in the absence of Brig Gen John B. Clark. *The Battle of Lexington, Fought in and Around the City of Lexington, Missouri, on September 18th, 19th and 20th, 1861, by Forces Under Command of Colonel James A. Mulligan, and General Sterling Price. The Official Records of Both Parties to the Conflict; to which is Added Memoirs of Participants*, (Lexington Historical Society, 1903), 59.
[374] Peterson et al, *Price's Lieutenants*, 164-69
[375] Peterson et al, *Price's Lieutenants*, 170
[376] Serving as mounted infantry, Peterson et al, *Price's Lieutenants*, 188
[377] Peterson et al, *Price's Lieutenants*, 188
[378] Peterson et al, *Price's Lieutenants*, 184
[379] Peterson et al, *Price's Lieutenants*, 163
[380] Commanded division in the absence of regular commander Brig Gen William Y. Slack who was likely recovering from his Wilson's Creek wound. *OR, Series I, Vol. III*, 186
[381] Peterson et al, *Price's Lieutenants*, 203; *OR, Series I, Vol. III*, 187
[382] Peterson et al, *Price's Lieutenants*, 209; Wood, *Lexington*, 59
[383] Peterson et al, *Price's Lieutenants*, 212-13

1st Missouri State Guard Cavalry: Lieutenant Colonel Louis C. Bohannon[384]
Missouri State Guard Cavalry Battalion: Lieutenant Colonel Richard Childs[385]

5th Division: Brigadier General Alexander E. Steen
    Colonel James P. Saunders[386]
1st Missouri State Guard: Colonel James P. Saunders
    Lieutenant Colonel James H. R. Cundiff[387]
3rd Missouri State Guard: Colonel Levin M. Lewis[388]
1st Missouri State Guard Battalion: Lieutenant Colonel John R. Boyd[389]
1st Missouri State Guard (Platte County) Battalion: Major John H. Winston[390]
2nd Missouri State Guard Cavalry: Lieutenant Colonel Redmond Wilfley[391]
1st Missouri State Guard Cavalry Battalion: Major John C. C. Thornton[392]
Kelly's (Irish) Light Artillery Battery: Captain Ephraim V. Kelly[393]

6th Division: Brigadier General Mosby Monroe Parsons[394]
1st Missouri State Guard: Captain John R. Champion[395]
2nd Missouri State Guard: Colonel George K. Dills (w)
    Lieutenant Colonel James K. Mitchell[396]
1st Missouri State Guard Cavalry: Colonel Robert McCulloch[397]
2nd Missouri State Guard Cavalry: Colonel Charles B. Alexander[398]
3rd Missouri State Guard Cavalry: Colonel James M. Johnson[399]
1st Missouri State Guard Light Artillery Battery: Captain Henry C. Guibor[400]

---

[384] Peterson et al, *Price's Lieutenants*, 196; *Battle of Lexington*, 54-55
[385] Peterson et al, *Price's Lieutenants*, 201
[386] Steen absent due to ill health, Saunders commanded in his absence *Battle of Lexington*, 49; *OR, Series I, Vol. III*, 187; Peterson et al, *Price's Lieutenants*, 217
[387] Peterson et al, *Price's Lieutenants*, 231; Wood, *Lexington*, 59
[388] Peterson et al, *Price's Lieutenants*, 238-40
[389] Peterson et al, *Price's Lieutenants*, 242
[390] Became 2nd Missouri State Guard Regiment September 23, Peterson et al, *Price's Lieutenants*, 238; *Battle of Lexington*, 64
[391] Peterson et al, *Price's Lieutenants*, 224; Wood, *Lexington*, 59
[392] Peterson et al, *Price's Lieutenants*, 229-30; *The Battle of Lexington*, 64-66
[393] Peterson et al, *Price's Lieutenants*, 247
[394] *The Battle of Lexington*, 41-46
[395] *Battle of Lexington*, 41; Wood, *Lexington*, 41, list Champion as in command of the regiment, however, Peterson et al, *Price's Lieutenants*,274, lists Champion only as commander of company B
[396] Dills "severely wounded by an accidental discharge, while gallantly leading his regiment." *Battle of Lexington*, 45; Allardice, *Confederate Colonels*, 425; Peterson et al, *Price's Lieutenants*, 276
[397] Peterson et al, *Price's Lieutenants*, 258; Wood, *Lexington*, 69
[398] Peterson et al, *Price's Lieutenants*,263; Wood, *Lexington*, 69
[399] Peterson et al, *Price's Lieutenants*,276
[400] Peterson et al, *Price's Lieutenants*, 285

7th Division: Brigadier General John H. McBride
1st Missouri State Guard: Colonel Edmund T. Wingo (w)
                Lieutenant Colonel Brigham F. Twigg[401]
2nd Missouri State Guard: Colonel Archibald A. MacFarlane[402]
1st Missouri State Guard Cavalry Battalion (Company E): Captain Leonidas St. Clair
    Campbell[403]

8th Division: Brigadier General James S. Rains
1st Missouri State Guard: Colonel Thomas H. Rosser[404]
2nd Missouri State Guard: Colonel Benjamin F. Elliott[405]
3rd Missouri State Guard: Colonel Edgar V.R. Hurst[406]
4th Missouri State Guard Battalion: Lieutenant Colonel Walter S. O'Kane[407]
5th Missouri State Guard: Colonel James J. Clarkson[408]
1st Missouri State Guard Cavalry (elements): Lieutenant Colonel John W. Martin[409]
2nd Missouri State Guard Cavalry: Colonel James C. McCown[410]
3rd Missouri State Guard Cavalry: Colonel Robert L.Y. Peyton[411]
4th Missouri State Guard Cavalry: Colonel Benjamin F. Walker[412]
5th Missouri State Guard Cavalry: Colonel Jeremiah C. Cravens[413]
6th Missouri State Guard Cavalry: Lieutenant Colonel John W. Payne
                Colonel John T. Coffee[414]
1st (Price's Rifles) Missouri State Guard Light Artillery Battery: Captain Emmett MacDonald
                                        Captain Hiram M. Bledsoe[415]
Clark's Light Artillery Battery: Captain Samuel Churchill Clark[416]

---

[401] Wingo wounded in the shoulder *Battle of Lexington*, 47; Peterson et al, *Price's Lieutenants*, 301
[402] Peterson et al, *Price's Lieutenants*, 303-06
[403] Peterson et al, *Price's Lieutenants*, 299-300
[404] Peterson et al, *Price's Lieutenants*, 321-29
[405] Peterson et al, *Price's Lieutenants*, 329-36
[406] Peterson et al, *Price's Lieutenants*, 336-41
[407] Peterson et al, *Price's Lieutenants*, 342-47
[408] Peterson et al, *Price's Lieutenants*, 347-51
[409] Peterson et al, *Price's Lieutenants*, 357-61
[410] Peterson et al, *Price's Lieutenants*, 361-67
[411] Peterson et al, *Price's Lieutenants*, 368-72
[412] Peterson et al, *Price's Lieutenants*, 372-76
[413] Peterson et al, *Price's Lieutenants*, 376-80
[414] Coffee assumed command September 16, Peterson et al, *Price's Lieutenants*, 380-85
[415] Bledsoe resumed command towards the end of the siege, *Lafayette County*, 346; Peterson et al, *Price's Lieutenants*, 410
[416] Peterson et al, *Price's Lieutenants*, 410

Liberty (Blue Mills Landing), Missouri
September 17, 1861

Union Forces[417]
Lieutenant Colonel John Scott

3rd Iowa (Detachment): Lieutenant Colonel John Scott
1 6 lb. gun: Captain Matthew M. Trumbull

Confederate Forces
Brigadier General David R. Atchison[418]

2nd Missouri State Guard (4th Division): Colonel Thomas Jefferson Patton[419]
Missouri State Guard Cavalry Battalion (4th Division): Lieutenant Colonel Richard Childs[420]
1st Missouri State Guard (5th Division): Colonel James P. Saunders[421]
1st Missouri State Guard Battalion (5th Division): Lieutenant Colonel John R. Boyd[422]
1st Missouri State Guard (Platte County) Battalion (5th Division): Major John H. Winston[423]
2nd Missouri State Guard Cavalry (5th Division): Lieutenant Colonel Redmond Wilfley[424]

---

[417] *OR Series I, Vol. III*, 193-94
[418] *OR Series I, Vol. III*, 195 for Atchison
[419] Peterson et al, *Price's Lieutenants*, 209
[420] Peterson et al, *Price's Lieutenants*, 201
[421] Peterson et al, *Price's Lieutenants*, 231
[422] Peterson et al, *Price's Lieutenants*, 242
[423] Peterson et al, *Price's Lieutenants*, 238
[424] Peterson et al, *Price's Lieutenants*, 224

Romney (Hanging Rock), West Virginia
September 23, 1861

Union Forces[425]

4th Ohio: Lieutenant Colonel John S. Mason[426]
8th Ohio: Colonel Herman G. Depuy[427]

Confederate Forces[428]
Colonel Angus W. McDonald

77th Virginia Militia: Colonel Edward H. McDonald[429]
114th Virginia Militia: Colonel Alexander Monroe (Moore)[430]
7th Virginia Cavalry: Major Oliver R. Funsten[431]
4-lb howitzer and 6-lb rifled gun: Lieutenant John H. Lionberger

---

[425] Phisterer, *Statistical Record*, 88
[426] *Ohio, Vol. 2*, 88-89
[427] *Ohio, Vol. 2*, 236-37
[428] *OR Series I, Vol. V*, 200-14
[429] Wallace, *Virginia*, 253-54
[430] Wallace, *Virginia*, 254 lists this officer as Alexander Moore
[431] Sifakis, *Confederate: Virginia*, 113

Greenbrier River, West Virginia
October 3, 1861

Union Forces[432]
Brigadier General Joseph J. Reynolds

24th Ohio: Colonel Jacob Ammen[433]
25th Ohio: Colonel John A. Jones [434]
32nd Ohio: Colonel Thomas H. Ford[435]
7th Indiana: Colonel James Gavin[436]
9th Indiana: Colonel Robert H. Milroy[437]
13th Indiana: Colonel Jeremiah C. Sullivan[438]
14th Indiana: Colonel Nathan Kimball[439]
15th Indiana: Colonel George D. Wagner[440]
17th Indiana: Colonel Milo S. Haskell[441]

Cavalry
1st Ohio Cavalry (Company A): Captain John H. Robinson[442]
Indiana Cavalry Company: Captain James R. Bracken[443]
Pennsylvania (Washington) Cavalry Company: Captain Andrew J. Greenfield[444]

Artillery
A, 1st Michigan Artillery: Captain Cyrus O. Loomis[445]
G, 4th United States Artillery: Captain Albion P. Howe
A, 1st West Virginia Artillery: Captain Philip Daum[446]

Confederate Forces[447]
Brigadier General Henry R. Jackson

---

[432] *OR, Series I, Vol. V,* 220-223
[433] *Ohio, Vol. 3,* 139
[434] *Ohio, Vol. 3,* 167
[435] *Ohio, Vol. 3,* 471
[436] *Indiana Vol. 2,* 40
[437] *Union, Vol. 3,* 112
[438] *Union, Vol. 3,* 116
[439] *Union, Vol. 3,* 117
[440] *Union, Vol. 3,* 118
[441] *Union, Vol. 3,* 119
[442] *Ohio, Vol. 11,* 5
[443] *Union, Vol. 3,* 128
[444] Samuel Clarke Farrar, *The Twenty Second Pennsylvania Cavalry and the Ringgold Battalion*, (Pittsburgh, Pa.: Twenty Second Pennsylvania Ringgold Cavalry Association, 1911), 23
[445] *Union, Vol. 3,* 429
[446] Union, Vol. 2, 308
[447] *OR Series I, Vol. V,* 224-36

1st Brigade: Colonel Albert Rust
3rd Arkansas: Lieutenant Colonel Seth M. Barton
31st Virginia: Lieutenant Colonel William L. Jackson
52nd Virginia: Colonel John F. Baldwin
9th Virginia Battalion: Captain John A. Robinson[448]
Cavalry Company: Captain George Jackson
5th Brigade: Colonel William B. Taliaferro
23rd Virginia: Lieutenant Colonel Alexander G. Taliaferro
25th Virginia: Captain John C. Higginbotham
37th Virginia: Colonel Samuel V. Fulkerson
44th Virginia: Colonel William C. Scott
Virginia (8th Star Artillery) Battery: Captain William H. Rice[449]
Virginia (Lynchburg "Lee" Artillery) Battery: Captain Pierce B. Anderson[450]
Virginia (Danville Artillery) Battery: Captain Lindsay M. Shumaker[451]

Johnson's Command: Colonel Edward Johnson
1st Georgia: Major George H. Thompson[452]
12th Georgia: Lieutenant Colonel Zephaniah T. Conner[453]

---

[448] Wallace, *Virginia*, 93
[449] Wise, *Long Arm Vol. 2*, 990
[450] *OR Series I, Vol. V*, 463
[451] Wise, *Long Arm Vol. 2*, 990
[452] Sifakis, *Confederate: South Carolina and Georgia*, 178
[453] Allardice, *Confederate Colonels*, 109

Santa Rosa Island, Florida
October 9, 1861

Union Forces[454]
Colonel Harvey Brown

9th New York: Colonel William Wilson
<u>Vodges' Command</u>: Major Israel Vodges (c)
        Captain John M. Hildt[455]
3rd United States (Company E): Captain John M. Hildt
3rd New York (Company G): Captain James H. Dobie[456]
A, 1st United States Artillery: Lieutenant Franck E. Taylor
<u>Arnold's Command</u>: Major. Lewis G. Arnold
3rd United States (Company C): Lieutenant Alexander M. Shipley
H, 2nd United States Artillery: Captain James M. Robertson

Confederate Forces[457]
Brigadier General Richard H. Anderson (w)[458]

Demolition Team (Homer's Artillery Company): Lieutenant James H. Hallonquist
<u>1st Battalion</u>: Colonel James R. Chalmers
Detachment, 10th Mississippi
Detachment, 1st Alabama
<u>2nd Battalion</u>: Colonel James Patton Anderson
3 companies, 7th Alabama
2 companies, Louisiana Infantry
2 companies, 1st Florida
<u>3rd Battalion</u>: Colonel John K. Jackson
Detachment, 5th Georgia
Detachment Georgia Artillery Battalion

---

[454] *OR Series I, Vol. VI*, 438-57
[455] *OR Series I, Vol. VI*, 439, for Vodges' capture and Hildt's assumption of command
[456] Phisterer, *New York*, 1782
[457] *OR Series I, Vol. VI*, 460-63-
[458] Wounded in the elbow, *OR Series I, Vol. VI*, 459

Fredericktown and Ironton, Missouri
October 17-21, 1861

Union Forces[459]
Colonel John B. Plummer[460]

<u>Carlin's Command</u>: Colonel William P. Carlin
21st Illinois: Colonel John W. S. Alexander
33rd Illinois: Colonel Charles E. Hovey
38th Illinois: Colonel William P. Carlin
8th Wisconsin: Colonel Robert C. Murphy[461]
1st Indiana Cavalry (6 companies): Colonel Conrad Baker
Missouri Cavalry Company: Captain Henry P. Hawkins[462]
<u>Plummer's Command</u>: Colonel John B. Plummer
17th Illinois: Colonel Leonard F. Ross
20th Illinois: Colonel Charles Carroll Marsh
11th Missouri: Lieutenant Colonel William E. Panabaker
Illinois Cavalry Company: Captain Warren Stewart
Missouri Cavalry Company: Captain Edward Langen
<u>Artillery</u>: Major John M. Schofield
1st Missouri Light Artillery Battery: Captain Francis H. Manter
2, 24-lb Howitzers: Lieutenant Charles W. Purcell[463]
B, 1st Illinois Artillery: Lieutenant Patrick H. White[464]

Confederate Forces
1st Division Missouri State Guard
Brigadier General Meriwether Jefferson Thompson

1st Missouri State Guard (1 Battalion): Major Claiborne E. Birthright[465]
2nd Missouri State Guard (1 Battalion): Lieutenant Colonel Benjamin J. Farmer[466]
3rd Missouri State Guard: Colonel Aden L. Lowe (k)
    Lieutenant Colonel Isaac N. Hedgepeth[467]

---

[459] *OR Series I, Vol. III*, 206-23
[460] Plummer had overall field command, *OR Series I, Vol. III,* 220
[461] *Wisconsin, Vol. 1,* 577
[462] *Annual Report of the Adjutant General of Missouri*, (Jefferson City: Emory S. Foster Public Printer, 1866), 345
[463] *Missouri,* 463
[464] *Illinois, Vol. 8,* 605
[465] Peterson et al, *Price's Lieutenants,* 77
[466] Peterson et al, *Price's Lieutenants,* 82
[467] Lowe shot through the head and killed instantly, See, *OR Series I, Vol. III, 233,* for this as well as Hedgepeth's succession; Peterson et al, *Price's Lieutenants,* 82-87

4th Missouri State Guard: Colonel Alexander Waugh[468]
1st Missouri State Guard Battalion: Lieutenant Colonel Thomas Brown[469]
2nd Missouri State Guard Battalion: Major Daniel Jennings[470]
3rd Missouri State Guard Battalion: Major William F. Rapley[471]
1st Missouri State Guard Cavalry: Lieutenant Colonel Edward A. Lewis[472]
2nd Missouri State Guard Cavalry: Colonel John J. Smith[473]
3rd Missouri State Guard Cavalry: Lieutenant Colonel James D. White[474]
Independent Missouri State Guard Cavalry Company: Captain Francis J. Smith[475]
Missouri State Guard Artillery Battery: Captain Samuel S. Harris[476]
Missouri State Guard Artillery Battery: Captain E. G. Richardson[477]

---

[468] Peterson et al, *Price's Lieutenants*, 88-92
[469] Peterson et al, *Price's Lieutenants*, 93-95
[470] Peterson et al, *Price's Lieutenants*, 95-96
[471] Peterson et al, *Price's Lieutenants*, 96-98
[472] Peterson et al, *Price's Lieutenants*, 59-62
[473] Peterson et al, *Price's Lieutenants*, 62-67
[474] Peterson et al, *Price's Lieutenants*, 67-71
[475] Peterson et al, *Price's Lieutenants*, 71
[476] Peterson et al, *Price's Lieutenants*, 99
[477] Peterson et al, *Price's Lieutenants*, 100

Ball's Bluff, Virginia[478]
October 21, 1861

Union Forces
Colonel Edward D. Baker (k)
Colonel William R. Lee
Colonel Milton Cogswell (w&c)[479]

15th Massachusetts: Colonel Charles Devens Jr.
20th Massachusetts: Colonel William R. Lee (c)
    Lieutenant Colonel Francis W. Palfrey[480]
42nd New York: Colonel Milton Cogswell
    Lieutenant Colonel James J. Mooney[481]
71st Pennsylvania: Lieutenant Colonel Isaac J. Wistar (w)[482]
B, 1st Rhode Island Artillery (1 gun): Lieutenant Walter M. Bramhall (w)[483]
I, 1st United States Artillery (2 guns): Lieutenant Frank S. French

Confederate Forces
Brigadier General Nathan G. Evans

17th Mississippi: Colonel Winfield S. Featherston
18th Mississippi: Colonel Erasmus R. Burt (mw)
    Lieutenant Colonel Thomas M. Griffin[484]
8th Virginia: Colonel Eppa Hunton
13th Mississippi (Company E): Captain Lorenzo D. Fletcher[485]
Virginia Cavalry (3 companies): Lieutenant Colonel Walter H. Jenifer

---

[478] *B&L Vol. 2,* 126

[479] Baker hit at least four times, including a fatal wound to the head. Charles Preston Poland, *Glories of War: Small Battles and Early Heroes of 1861,* (AuthorHouse, 2006), 147. Lee assumed command upon Baker's death yielded command to Cogswell as he was the senior officer. *OR Series I, Vol. V,* 297. Cogswell wounded in the hand and taken prisoner. See *OR Series I, Vol. V,* 325

[480] See *OR Series I, Vol. V,* 318, 320 for Lee and Palfrey

[481] See *OR Series I, Vol. V,* 326 for Mooney

[482] Wounded 3 times in jaw, thigh, and right elbow. Poland, *Glories of War,* 146

[483] See *OR Series I, Vol. V,* 322

[484] Wounded in the abdomen and died October 26, 1861. Bradley M. Gottfried, *The Maps of Bull Run,* (New York: Savas Beattie LLC, 2009), 96

[485] Dick Stanley, "Captain Lorenzo Dow Fletcher," *13th Mississippi Infantry Regiment,* (July 11, 2015). Accessed December 22, 2015, http://13thmississippi.com/2015/07/11/captain-lorenzo-dow-fletcher/

Camp Wildcat (Rockcastle Hills), Kentucky[486]
October 21, 1861

Union Forces[487]
Brigadier General Albin F. Schoepf

33rd Indiana (Companies D, E, & G): Colonel John Coburn
7th Kentucky: Colonel Theophilus T. Garrard
14th Ohio (Companies B, C, & G): Colonel James B. Steedman
17th Ohio (Companies C, E, H, & K): Colonel John M. Connell
1st Kentucky Cavalry: Colonel Frank Wolford
B, 1st Ohio Light Artillery: Captain William B. Standart

Confederate Forces
Brigadier General Felix K. Zolicoffer

15th Mississippi: Colonel Winfield S. Statham[488]
11th Tennessee: Colonel James E. Rains
17th Tennessee: Colonel Tazewell W. Newman[489]
20th Tennessee: Colonel Joel A. Battle[490]
19th Tennessee: Colonel David H. Cummings[491]
1st Tennessee Cavalry Battalion: Lieutenant Colonel Frank N. McNairy[492]
2nd (3rd) Tennessee Cavalry Battalion: Lieutenant Colonel William N. Brazelton Jr.[493]
Tennessee (Rutledge's) Battery: Captain Arthur M. Rutledge[494]

---

[486] J.H. Battle, W.H. Perrin, G.C. Kniffin, *Kentucky: A History of the State*, (Louisville, Ky., Chicago, Ill.: F.A. Battery Publishing Company, 1885), 373-78; Randy Bishop, *Kentucky's Civil War Battlefields: A Guide to Their History and Preservation*, (Pelican Publishing Company Inc., 2012), 33-45
[487] *OR Series I, Vol. IV,* 208-09,; Phisterer, *Statistical Record*, 89
[488] Allardice, *Confederate Colonels*, 355
[489] *OR Series I, Vol. IV,* 213-14
[490] John Berrien Lindsley, Ed., *The Military Annals of Tennessee: Confederate*, (Nashville: J.M. Lindsley and Company Publishers, 1866), 388-93
[491] Lindsley, Ed., *Tennessee*, 372-73
[492] Sifakis, *Confederate: Tennessee*, 37
[493] Sifakis, *Confederate: Tennessee*, 42
[494] Sibley, *Confederate Artillery Organizations*, 230

Belmont, Missouri
November 7, 1861

Union Forces[495]
Brigadier General Ulysses S. Grant

1st Brigade: Brigadier General John A. McClernand
27th Illinois: Colonel Napoleon B. Buford
30th Illinois: Colonel Philip B. Fouke
31st Illinois: Colonel John A. Logan
2nd Illinois Cavalry (Company L): Lieutenant James K. Catlin[496]
15th Illinois Cavalry (Company B): Captain James J. Dollins[497]
B, 1st Illinois Light Artillery: Captain Ezra Taylor
2nd Brigade: Colonel Henry Dougherty (w&c)[498]
22nd Illinois: Lieutenant Colonel Harrison E. Hart
7th Iowa: Colonel Jacob G. Lauman
Gun-Boats
U.S.S. Lexington: Captain Roger N. Stembel[499]
U.S.S. Tyler: Captain Henry Walke

Confederate Forces[500]
Major General Leonidas Polk

1st Division: Brigadier General Gideon J. Pillow
1st Brigade: Colonel Joseph Knox Walker[501]
2nd Tennessee: Lieutenant Colonel William B. Ross
13th Tennessee: Colonel John V. Wright
15th Tennessee: Colonel Charles M. Carroll[502]
Tennessee (Polk's) Battery: Captain Marshall T. Polk[503]
2nd Brigade: Colonel Robert M. Russell

---

[495] *B&L, Vol. 1,* 355
[496] *Illinois Vol. 7,* 519
[497] *Illinois Vol. 8,* 494
[498] Wounded 3 times in the shoulder, elbow, and ankle and subsequently taken prisoner. *OR Series I, Vol. III,* 293
[499] Officers of the Continental and U.S. Navy and Marine Corps 1775-1900, "Navy Officers 1798-1900, S," *Naval History and Heritage Command.* Accessed February 26, 2014. http://www.history.navy.mil/browse-by-topic/organization-and-administration/historical-leadership/navy-and-marine-corps-officers-1775-1900.html
[500] *B&L, Vol. 1,* 355-56; *OR Series I, Vol. III,* 723-24
[501] Allardice, *Confederate Colonels,* 383
[502] Attached to Marks' Brigade during the battle. Nathaniel Cheairs Hughes, *The Battle of Belmont: Grant Strikes South,* (University of North Carolina Press, 1991), 134-35
[503] Sibley, *Confederate Artillery Organizations,* 215

12th Tennessee: Lieutenant Colonel Tyree H. Bell
21st Tennessee: Colonel Edward Pickett Jr.
22nd Tennessee: Colonel Thomas J. Freeman
Tennessee (Jackson's) Battery: Captain William H. Jackson (w)
                             Lieutenant William W. Carnes[504]

<u>3rd Brigade</u>: Colonel William E. Travis[505]
9th Arkansas: Colonel John M. Bradley[506]
13th Arkansas: Colonel James C. Tappan[507]
5th Tennessee: Lieutenant Colonel John D. Atkins[508]

<u>Division Cavalry</u>
6th Tennessee Cavalry Battalion: Lieutenant Colonel Thomas H. Logwood[509]

<u>Division Artillery</u>
Tennessee (Southern Guards Artillery [Memphis Southern Guards Artillery]): Captain S. H. D. Hamilton[510]

2nd Division: Brigadier General Benjamin F. Cheatham
<u>1st Brigade</u>: Colonel Preston Smith[511]
154th Senior Tennessee: Lieutenant Colonel Marcus J. Wright
1st Mississippi Battalion: Lieutenant Colonel Andrew K. Blythe[512]
Mississippi (Pettus Flying Artillery) Battery: Captain Alfred Hudson[513]

<u>2nd Brigade</u>: Colonel William H. Stephens[514]
6th Tennessee: Lieutenant Colonel Timothy P. Jones[515]
9th Tennessee: Colonel Henry L. Douglass[516]
Mississippi (Smith's) Battery: Captain Melancthon Smith[517]

<u>Division Cavalry</u>
1st Mississippi Cavalry Battalion: Lieutenant Colonel John H. Miller[518]

---

[504] Sibley, *Confederate Artillery Organizations*, 115-16; *OR Series I, Vol. III*, 329 for Jackson's wounding
[505] Brigade not engaged, across the river at Columbus, *Tennesseans in the Civil War Volume 1*, (Nashville: Civil War Centennial Commission, 1964), 184-85
[506] Allardice, *Confederate Colonels*, 72
[507] Attached to Russell's Brigade during the battle, *Tennesseans in the Civil War Volume 1*, 199
[508] *Tennesseans in the Civil War Volume 1*, 184-85
[509] Sifakis, *Confederate: Tennessee*, 48-49
[510] Sibley, *Confederate Artillery Organizations*, 256
[511] *Tennesseans in the Civil War Volume 1*, 310
[512] Sifakis, *Confederate: Mississippi*, 67
[513] Sibley, *Confederate Artillery Organizations*, 213
[514] *Tennesseans in the Civil War Volume 1*, 186-87, Not actively engaged in battle
[515] *Tennesseans in the Civil War Volume 1*, 186-87
[516] *Tennesseans in the Civil War Volume 1*, 192-93
[517] Sibley, *Confederate Artillery Organizations*, 235
[518] Sifakis, *Confederate: Mississippi*, 31

3rd Division: Brigadier General John P. McCown
1st Brigade: Colonel Samuel F. Marks[519]
5th Louisiana Battalion: Lieutenant Colonel John B.G. Kennedy[520]
11th Louisiana: Lieutenant Colonel Robert H. Barrow[521]
Tennessee (Bankhead's [Company B, 1st Tennessee Light Artillery]) Battery: Captain Smith P. Bankhead[522]
2nd Brigade: Colonel Rufus P. Neely[523]
4th Tennessee: Lieutenant Colonel Otho F. Strahl[524]
12th Louisiana: Colonel Thomas M. Scott[525]
Mississippi (Point Coupee Artillery) Battery: Captain Richard A. Stewart[526]
Division Cavalry[527]
Mississippi Cavalry Company: Captain Clement L. Hudson[528]
Tennessee Cavalry Company: Captain Robert Haywood
Tennessee Cavalry Company: Captain James J. Neely

4th Division: Colonel John S. Bowen[529]
1st Brigade: Colonel John D. Martin
25th Mississippi: Lieutenant Colonel Edward F. McGhee[530]
1st Missouri: Lieutenant Colonel Lucius L. Rich[531]
Mississippi (Watson) Battery: Captain Daniel M. Beltzhoover[532]
2nd Brigade: Colonel DeWitt C. Bonham[533]
10th Arkansas: Colonel Thomas D. Merrick
22nd Mississippi: Lieutenant Colonel Frank Schaller[534]
Tennessee (Memphis Light) Battery: Captain William O. Williams[535]
Division Cavalry[536]

---

[519] Hughes, *The Battle of Belmont*, 134-35
[520] Arthur W. Bergeron Jr., *A Guide to Louisiana Confederate Military Units 1861-1865*, (LSU Press, 1989), 159; Sifakis, *Confederate: Louisiana*, 75
[521] Bergeron, *Louisiana*, 98
[522] Sibley, *Confederate Artillery Organizations*, 27
[523] Not engaged, across the river at Columbus, *Tennesseans in the Civil War Volume 1*, 182-84
[524] *Tennesseans in the Civil War Volume 1*, 182-84
[525] Bergeron, *Louisiana*, 99
[526] Sibley, *Confederate Artillery Organizations*, 214
[527] Not Engaged; *OR Series I, Vol. III*, 699
[528] Dunbar Rowland, *The Official and Statistical Record of the State of Mississippi 1908*, (Nashville: Brandon Printing Company, 1908), 762-63
[529] Infantry and Cavalry not engaged
[530] Sifakis, *Confederate: Mississippi*, 114
[531] Sifakis, *Confederate: Mississippi*, 111
[532] Sibley, *Confederate Artillery Organizations*, 313
[533] Allardice, *Confederate Colonels*, 65
[534] Allardice, *Confederate Colonels*, 334
[535] Sibley, *Confederate Artillery Organizations*, 315-16

Alabama Cavalry Company: Captain Jefferson L. Faulkner[537]
Alabama Cavalry Company: Captain Alexander W. Bowie[538]
Mississippi Cavalry Company: Captain Warren Colonele

Heavy Artillery: Major Alexander P. Stewart
Tennessee (Company F, 1st Tennessee Heavy Artillery) Battery: Captain Andrew Jackson Jr.[539]
Tennessee (Company E, 1st Tennessee Heavy Artillery) Battery: Captain Robert Sterling[540]
Tennessee (Company C, 1st Tennessee Light Artillery) Battery: Captain William Y. C. Humes[541]

---

[536] *OR Series I, Vol. III,* 699
[537] Brewer, *Alabama,* 692
[538] Brewer, *Alabama,* 692
[539] Sibley, *Confederate Artillery Organizations,* 272
[540] Sibley, *Confederate Artillery Organizations,* 260
[541] Sibley, *Confederate Artillery Organizations,* 111-12

Port Royal (Fort's Beauregard and Walker), South Carolina
November 7, 1861

Union Forces[542]
Brigadier General Thomas W. Sherman

<u>1st Brigade</u>: Brigadier General Egbert L. Viele
8th Maine: Colonel Lee Strickland
3rd New Hampshire: Colonel Enoch Q. Fellows
46th New York: Colonel Rudolph Rosa
47th New York: Colonel Henry Moore
48th New York: Colonel James H. Perry
<u>2nd Brigade</u>: Brigadier General Isaac I. Stevens
8th Michigan: Colonel William M. Fenton
79th New York: Lieutenant Colonel William H. Nobels
50th Pennsylvania: Colonel Benjamin C. Christ
100th Pennsylvania: Colonel Daniel Leasure
<u>3rd Brigade</u>: Brigadier General Horatio G. Wright
6th Connecticut: Colonel John L. Chatfield
7th Connecticut: Colonel Alfred H. Terry
9th Maine: Colonel Rishworth Rich
4th New Hampshire: Colonel Thomas J. Whipple
<u>Unattached</u>
3rd Rhode Island: Colonel Nathaniel W. Brown
1st New York Engineers: Colonel Edward W. Serrell
E, 3rd United States Artillery: Captain John Hamilton

Union Naval Forces[543]
South-Atlantic Blockading Squadron
Flag Officer Samuel H. DuPont & Captain Charles H. Davis (Fleet Captain)

<u>Frigates</u>
Flag-Ship U.S.S. Wabash: Commander Christopher R. P. Rogers[544]
<u>Side-Wheel Steamers</u>
U.S.S. Susquehanna: Captain James L. Lardiner[545]

---

[542] *B&L, Vol. 1*, 691
[543] *B&L, Vol. 1*, 691
[544] Officers of the Continental and U.S. Navy and Marine Corps 1775-1900, "Navy Officers 1798-1900, R," *Naval History and Heritage Command*. Accessed February 26, 2014. http://www.history.navy.mil/browse-by-topic/organization-and-administration/historical-leadership/navy-and-marine-corps-officers-1775-1900.html

Sloops
U.S.S. Mohican: Commander Sylvanus W. Gordon
U.S.S. Pocahontas: Commander Percival Drayton
U.S.S. Pawnee: Lieutenant Robert H. Wyman[546]
U.S.S. Seminole: Commander John P. Gillis[547]

Gunboats
U.S.S. Unadilla: Lieutenant Napoleon Collins
U.S.S. Seneca: Lieutenant Daniel Ammen
U.S.S. Ottawa: Lieutenant Thomas H. Stevens[548]
U.S.S. Pembina: Lieutenant John P. Bankhead[549]

Sailing Sloops
U.S.S. Augusta: Commander Enoch G. Parrott[550]
U.S.S. Bienville: Commander Charles Steedman
U.S.S. Curlew: Lieutenant Pendleton G. Watmaugh
U.S.S. Isaac Smith: Lieutenant James W.A. Nicholson[551]
U.S.S. Penguin: Lieutenant Thomas A. Budd[552]
U.S.S. R.B. Forbes: Lieutenant Henry S. Newcomb[553]
U.S.S. Vanadalia: Commander Francis S. Haggerty[554]

---

[545] Officers of the Continental and U.S. Navy and Marine Corps 1775-1900, "Navy Officers 1798-1900, L," *Naval History and Heritage Command*. Accessed February 26, 2014. http://www.history.navy.mil/browse-by-topic/organization-and-administration/historical-leadership/navy-and-marine-corps-officers-1775-1900.html

[546] Officers of the Continental and U.S. Navy and Marine Corps 1775-1900, "Navy Officers 1798-1900, W," *Naval History and Heritage Command*. Accessed February 26, 2014. http://www.history.navy.mil/browse-by-topic/organization-and-administration/historical-leadership/navy-and-marine-corps-officers-1775-1900.html

[547] Officers of the Continental and U.S. Navy and Marine Corps 1775-1900, "Navy Officers 1798-1900, G," *Naval History and Heritage Command*. Accessed February 26, 2014. http://www.history.navy.mil/browse-by-topic/organization-and-administration/historical-leadership/navy-and-marine-corps-officers-1775-1900.html

[548] Dictionary of American Naval Fighting Ships, "Ottawa," *Naval History and Heritage Command*. Accessed February 26, 2014. http://www.history.navy.mil/research/histories/ship-histories/danfs.html

[549] Dictionary of American Naval Fighting Ships, "Pembina," *Naval History and Heritage Command*. Accessed February 26, 2014. http://www.history.navy.mil/research/histories/ship-histories/danfs.html

[550] Dictionary of American Naval Fighting Ships, "Augusta," *Naval History and Heritage Command*. Accessed February 26, 2014. http://www.history.navy.mil/research/histories/ship-histories/danfs.html

[551] Officers of the Continental and U.S. Navy and Marine Corps 1775-1900, "Navy Officers 1798-1900, N," *Naval History and Heritage Command*. Accessed February 26, 2014. http://www.history.navy.mil/browse-by-topic/organization-and-administration/historical-leadership/navy-and-marine-corps-officers-1775-1900.html

[552] Dictionary of American Naval Fighting Ships, "Penguin," *Naval History and Heritage Command*. Accessed February 26, 2014. http://www.history.navy.mil/research/histories/ship-histories/danfs.html

[553] Officers of the Continental and U.S. Navy and Marine Corps 1775-1900, "Navy Officers 1798-1900, N," *Naval History and Heritage Command*. Accessed February 26, 2014. http://www.history.navy.mil/browse-by-topic/organization-and-administration/historical-leadership/navy-and-marine-corps-officers-1775-1900.html

[554] Officers of the Continental and U.S. Navy and Marine Corps 1775-1900, "Navy Officers 1798-1900, H," *Naval History and Heritage Command*. Accessed February 26, 2014. http://www.history.navy.mil/browse-by-topic/organization-and-administration/historical-leadership/navy-and-marine-corps-officers-1775-1900.html

Confederate Forces[555]
Brigadier General Thomas F. Drayton

Fort Walker: Colonel William C. Heyward
4th Georgia Battalion: Lieutenant Colonel William H. Stiles Jr.[556]
9th [11th] South Carolina (3 companies): Colonel William C. Heyward
15th South Carolina: Colonel Wilmot G. DeSaussure
1st South Carolina Militia Artillery (Companies A and B): Colonel John A. Wagoner (w)
                                                                Major Arthur M. Huger[557]

Fort Beauregard: Colonel Richard G. M. Dunovant
9th [11th] South Carolina (Company D): Captain John J. Harrison [558]
12th South Carolina (6 companies): Colonel Richard G. M. Dunovant
Beaufort (South Carolina) Guerillas: Captain John H. Screvens[559]
Georgia (Read's) Battery: Captain Jacob Read[560]
South Carolina (Beaufort Artillery) Battery: Captain Stephen Elliott Jr. (w)
                                                                Lieutenant Hal M. Stuart[561]

Confederate Naval Forces[562]
Flag Officer Josiah Tattnall

C.S.S. Savannah (Flag-Ship): Lieutenant John N. Maffit
C.S.S. Sampson: Lieutenant Joel S. Kennard[563]
C.S.S. Resolute: Lieutenant J. Pembroke Jones

---

[555] *B&L, Vol. 1*, 691; *OR Series I, Vol. VI,* 6-30
[556] Sifakis, *Confederate: South Carolina and Georgia*, 187
[557] Wagoner stunned by a shell and Huger assumed command, *OR Series I, Vol. VI*, 17; Seigler, *South Carolina, Vol. 4*, 263-64, 268
[558] Seigler, *South Carolina Vol. 1*, 110
[559] Seigler, *South Carolina, Vol. 4*, 257
[560] Sibley, *Confederate Artillery Organizations*, 220
[561] Wounded in the leg by a shell fragment. *OR Series I, Vol. VI*, 29; Seigler, *South Carolina Vol. 1*. 268
[562] *B& L, Vol. 1* 691
[563] Officers of the Continental and U.S. Navy and Marine Corps 1775-1900, "Navy Officers 1798-1900, K," *Naval History and Heritage Command*. Accessed February 26, 2014. http://www.history.navy.mil/browse-by-topic/organization-and-administration/historical-leadership/navy-and-marine-corps-officers-1775-1900.html

Ivy Mountain (Piketown), Kentucky
November 8-9, 1861

Union Forces[564]
Colonel Joshua W. Sill

2nd Ohio: Colonel Leonard A. Harris
21st Ohio: Colonel Jesse S. Norton
33rd Ohio: Colonel Joshua W. Sill
59th Ohio: Colonel James P. Fyffe
Kentucky Volunteer Battalion: Colonel Charles A. Marshall
2 companies, Kentucky Volunteers: Colonel Leonidas K. Metcalfe
Kentucky Volunteers Command (35 men): Colonel Richard Apperson[565]

Confederate Forces[566]

5th Kentucky: Colonel John S. Williams[567]
1st Kentucky Cavalry Battalion: Major Jonathan Shawhan[568]

---

[564] Phisterer, *Statistical Record*, 90; *OR Series I, Vol. IV*, 225-27
[565] Captain Thomas Speed, Col R. M. Kelly, and Major Alfred Pirtle, *The Union Regiments of Kentucky*, (Louisville, Kentucky: Courier-Journal Job Printing Company, 1897), 526
[566] *OR Series I, Vol. IV*, 227-30; Evans, ed. *CMH Vol. 9, "Kentucky,"* 45
[567] Sifakis, *Confederate: Kentucky, Maryland, Missouri, The Confederate Units, and the Indian Units*, 37-38
[568] Sifakis, *Confederate: Kentucky, Maryland, Missouri, The Confederate Units, and the Indian Units*, 10

Pensacola (Fort Pickens), Florida
November 23, 1861

Union Forces[569]
Colonel Harvey Brown

Overall Commander of the Batteries
Major Lewis G. Arnold

Fort Pickens: Major Lewis G. Arnold
6th New York (Company D): Captain Patrick Duffy[570]
6th New York (Company H): Captain Charles E. Heuberer[571]
3rd United States (Company C): Lieutenant Alexander M. Shipley
3rd United States (Company E): Captain John M. Hildt
1, 10-inch Columbiad (Detachment, C, 2nd U.S. Artillery): Lieutenant Walter McFarland[572]
A, 1st United States Artillery: Captain Samuel F. Chalfin
L, 1st United States Artillery: Lieutenant Richard H. Jackson
K, 2nd United States Artillery: Captain Harvey A. Allen
Ditch (Mortar) Battery: Lieutenant Loomis L. Langdon
Battery Lincoln: Captain James M. Robertson
6th New York (Company G): Captain James H. Dobie[573]
H, 2nd United States Artillery: Captain James M. Robertson
Battery Cameron: Lieutenant Alexander C. M. Pennington
Company I, 6th New York (Company I): Captain Robert Bailey[574]
2nd United States Artillery (Detachment): Lieutenant Alexander C. M. Pennington
Battery Totten: Captain Matthew M. Blunt
C, 2nd United States Artillery: Captain Matthew M. Blunt
Battery Scott: Captain Richard C. Duryea
F, 1st United States Artillery: Lieutenant Henry W. Closson[575]
Spanish Fort Battery: Lieutenant Francis W. Seeley
6th New York (Company K): Lieutenant Jacob Silloway[576]
K, 2nd United States Artillery (Detachment): Lieutenant Francis W. Seeley

---

[569] *OR Series I, Vol. VI,* 469-88
[570] Phisterer, *New York,* 1781
[571] Phisterer, *New York,* 1782
[572] *Official Army Register for September 1861,* (Adjutant Generals Office, 1861), 17
[573] Phisterer, *New York,* 1782
[574] Phisterer, *New York,* 1782
[575] *Official Army Register,* 27
[576] Phisterer, *New York,* 1782

Union Naval Forces[577]
Flag Officer William McKean

U.S.S. Niagara: Flag Officer William McKean
U.S.S. Hartford [Richmond]: Captain Francis B. Ellison[578]

Confederate Forces[579]
Army of Pensacola
Major General Braxton Bragg

1st Brigade: Brigadier General Adley H. Gladden
1st Alabama: Colonel Henry D. Clayton
17th Alabama: Colonel Thomas H. Watts[580]
1st Georgia Battalion: Colonel John B. Villepigue (w)[581]
5th Georgia: Colonel John K. Jackson
9th Mississippi: Colonel James R. Chalmers
10th Mississippi: Colonel Robert A. Smith[582]
2nd Brigade: Brigadier General Richard H. Anderson
1st Florida: Colonel James Patton Anderson
1st Louisiana: Colonel Daniel W. Adams
Detachment, Confederate States Marines: Captain Alfred C. Van Benthuysen[583]
Artillery:
Battery #1: Captain S. S. Batchelor
Battery #2: Captain J. T. Wheat
Mortar Battery: Lieutenant G. W. Mader

---

[577] *OR Series I, Vol. VI*, 469
[578] *OR Series I, Vol. VI*, 490
[579] *OR Series I, Vol. VI*, 488-95, 762, 819
[580] Ilene D. Thompson, Wilbur E. Thompson, *The Seventeenth Alabama: A Regimental History and Roster*, (Heritage Books, 2001), 11
[581] "Severely wounded by a splinter "during bombardment. *OR Series I, Vol. VI*, 472
[582] Rowland, *Mississippi*, 595, 599
[583] Arthur Wyllie, *Confederate Officers*, (N.P., 2007), 522

Camp Alleghany (Buffalo Mountain), West Virginia
December 13, 1861

Union Forces[584]
Brigadier General Robert H. Milroy

9th Indiana: Colonel Gideon C. Moody[585]
13th Indiana: Colonel Jeremiah C. Sullivan[586]
25th Ohio: Colonel John A. Jones
32nd Ohio: Colonel Thomas H. Ford[587]
2nd West Virginia: Colonel John W. Moss[588]

Confederate Forces[589]
Colonel Edward Johnson

12th Georgia: Lieutenant Colonel Zephaniah T. Conner
9th Virginia Battalion: Lieutenant Colonel George W. Hansbrough (w)
    Major Gideon D. Camden Jr.[590]
25th Virginia: Major Albert G. Reger[591]
31st Virginia: Major Francis M. Boykin Jr.[592]
52nd Virginia: Major John D. H. Ross[593]
Pittsylvania Cavalry: Lieutenant Chiswell E. Dabney
Virginia (Lynchburg "Lee" Artillery) Battery: Captain Pierce B. Anderson (k)
    Lieutenant Charles I. Raine[594]
Virginia (2nd Rockbridge Artillery) Battery: Captain John Miller[595]

---

[584] Phisterer, *Statistical Record*, 92; *OR Series I, Vol. V*, 456-58
[585] *Union, Vol. 3*, 112
[586] *Union, Vol. 3*, 116
[587] *Ohio, Vol. 3*, 471
[588] *OR, Series I, Vol. V*, 185; *Union, Vol. 2*, 300
[589] *OR Series I, Vol. V*, 460-68
[590] Hansbrough wounded by a pistol shot to the thigh. *OR Series I, Vol. V*, 466; Wallace, *Virginia*, 93
[591] Sifakis, *Confederate: Virginia*, 206
[592] Sifakis, *Confederate: Virginia*, 217-18
[593] Sifakis, *Confederate: Virginia*, 244
[594] See, *OR Series I, Vol. V*, 463 for Anderson's death; Sibley, *Confederate Artillery Organizations*, 126
[595] Oren Frederic Morton, *A History of Rockbridge County Virginia*, (McClure Company, 1920), 411

Rowlett's Station (Mumfordsville, Woodsonville), Kentucky
December 17, 1861

Union Forces[596]

32nd Indiana: Colonel August Willich & Lieutenant Colonel Henry Von Trebra[597]

Confederate Forces[598]
Brigadier General Thomas C. Hindman

1st Arkansas: Colonel John S. Marmaduke
2nd Arkansas: Colonel Daniel C. Govan[599]
8th Texas Cavalry (1st Texas Rangers): Colonel Benjamin F. Terry (k)
                                               Lieutenant Colonel Samuel P. Christian[600]
Mississippi (Warren Light Artillery) Battery: Captain Charles M. Swett[601]

---

[596] *OR Series I, Vol. VII*, 14-19, 501
[597] *Union, Vol. 3*, 130-31
[598] *OR Series I, Vol. VII*, 19-21, 501
[599] Sifakis, *Confederate: Florida and Arkansas*, 71
[600] See, *OR Series I, Vol. VII*, 20 for Terry; Stephen B. Oates, *Confederate Cavalry, West of the River*, (University of Texas Press, 2010), 174; Sifakis, *Confederate: Texas*, 59
[601] Sibley, *Confederate Artillery Organizations*, 308

Dranesville, Virginia
December 20, 1861

Union Forces[602]
Brigadier General Edward O. C. Ord

1st Pennsylvania Reserve Rifles: Lieutenant Colonel Thomas L. Kane (w)[603]
6th Pennsylvania Reserves: Lieutenant Colonel William H. Penrose
9th Pennsylvania Reserves: Colonel Conrad Feger Jackson
10th Pennsylvania Reserves: Colonel John S. McCalmont
12th Pennsylvania Reserves: Colonel John H. Taggart
1st Pennsylvania Cavalry (2 squadrons): Lieutenant Colonel Jacob C. Higgins
A, 1st Pennsylvania Reserves Light Artillery: Captain Hezekiah Easton

Confederate Forces[604]
Brigadier General James E. B. Stuart

10th Alabama: Colonel John H. Forney (w)
        Lieutenant Colonel James B. Martin (k)
        Major John J. Woodward (w)[605]
1st Kentucky: Colonel Thomas H. Taylor
6th South Carolina: Lieutenant Colonel Andrew J. Secrest[606]
11th Virginia: Colonel Samuel Garland Jr.
1st North Carolina Cavalry (100 men): Major James B. Gordon
2nd Virginia Cavalry (50 men): Captain Andrew L. Pitzer
Georgia (Sumter Flying Artillery) Battery: Captain Allen S. Cutts[607]

---

[602] Phisterer, *Statistical Record*, 92; *OR Series I, Vol. V*, 473-89
[603] Wounded in the face, Welsh, *Medical Histories of Union Generals*, 186; *OR Series I, Vol. V*, 480
[604] *OR Series I, Vol. V*, 475, 490-94
[605] Forney "Severely wounded in the arm" Evans, *CMH Vol. 7 "Alabama,"* 406. Evans, *CMH Vol. 7 "Alabama,"* 88 for Martin. See, *OR Series I, Vol. V*, 491, 493 for Woodward.; Sifakis, *Confederate: Alabama*, 69-70
[606] Seigler, *South Carolina Vol. 2*, 138
[607] Sibley, *Confederate Artillery Organizations*, 265

Bibliography

Allardice, Bruce S. *Confederate Colonels: A Biographical Register*. Columbia Mo.: University of Missouri Press, 2008

Allardice, Bruce S. *More Generals in Gray*. Louisiana State University Press, 1995

Annual Report of the Adjutant General of Missouri. Jefferson City: Emory S. Foster Public Printer, 1866

Annual report of the adjutant general of Rhode Island and Providence Plantations, for the year 1865. Providence: E.L. Freeman and Son, 1893-95

Arrington, Bobby Lee. "Confederate Units Militia," *West Virginia The Other History*. Accessed December 6, 2014. https://sites.google.com/site/wvotherhistory/confederate-units-militia

Bates, Samuel P. *History of Pennsylvania Volunteers, 1861-65*. Harrisburg: B. Singerly, 1869. 5 Vols.

Battle, J.H. W.H. Perrin, G.C. Kniffin. *Kentucky: A History of the State*. Louisville, Ky., Chicago, Ill.: F.A. Battery Publishing Company, 1885

Bergeron, Arthur W. Jr. *A Guide to Louisiana Confederate Military Units 1861-1865*. LSU Press, 1989

Bishop, Randy. *Kentucky's Civil War Battlefields: A Guide to Their History and Preservation*. Pelican Publishing Company Inc., 2012

Boatner, Mark M. III. *The Civil War Dictionary*. New York: David McKay Company, Inc., 1959

Boyle, Esmerelda *Biographical Sketches of Distinguished Marylanders*. Baltimore: Kelly, Piet, & Company, 1877

Brewer, Willis. *Alabama, Her History, Resources, War Record, and Public Men: From 1540 to 1872.* Montgomery: Barrett & Brown Steam Printers and Book Binders, 1872

Brown, Kent Masterson. *The Civil War In Kentucky: The Battle for the Bluegrass State.* DaCapo Press, 2000

Carnes, Eva Margaret ed. *Centennial History of the Philippi Covered Bridge, 1852-1952.* Barbour County Historical Society, 1952

Chance, Joseph E. *The Second Texas Infantry: From Shiloh to Vicksburg.* Eakin Press, 1984

Cobb, Vicky Layton. *Ozark Pioneers.* Arcadia Publishing, 2001.

Connecticut Adjutant General's Office. *Catalogue of Connecticut Volunteer Organizations, (infantry, Cavalry, and Artillery,) in the Service of the United States, 1861-1865.* Brown and Gross, 1869

Davis, Nicholas A. and Donald E. Everett, eds. *Chaplain Davis and Hood's Texas Brigade: Being an Expanded Edition of the Reverend Nicholas A. Davis's The Campaign from Texas to Maryland, with The Battle of Fredericksburg.* Louisiana State University Press, 1962

Davis, William C. *Battle at Bull Run.* New York: Doubleday, 1977

Dickert, D. Augustus. *History of Kershaw's Brigade.* Elbert H. Aull Company, 1899

Dictionary of American Naval Fighting Ships, "Augusta," *Naval History and Heritage Command.* Accessed February 26, 2014. http://www.history.navy.mil/research/histories/ship-histories/danfs.html

Dictionary of American Naval Fighting Ships, "Minnesota," *Naval History and Heritage Command.* Accessed February 26, 2014. http://www.history.navy.mil/research/histories/ship-histories/danfs.html

Dictionary of American Naval Fighting Ships, "Ottawa," *Naval History and Heritage Command.* Accessed February 26, 2014. http://www.history.navy.mil/research/histories/ship-histories/danfs.html

Dictionary of American Naval Fighting Ships, "Pembina," *Naval History and Heritage Command.* Accessed February 26, 2014. http://www.history.navy.mil/research/histories/ship-histories/danfs.html

Dictionary of American Naval Fighting Ships, "Penguin," *Naval History and Heritage Command.* Accessed February 26, 2014. http://www.history.navy.mil/research/histories/ship-histories/danfs.html

Dictionary of American Naval Fighting Ships, "Whitehall," *Naval History and Heritage Command.* Accessed February 26, 2014. http://www.history.navy.mil/research/histories/ship-histories/danfs.html

Doubleday, Abner. *Reminiscences of Forts Sumter and Moultrie in 1860-61.* Harper and Brothers, 1876

Dyer, Frederick H. *A Compendium of the War of the Rebellion Volume 1: Number and Organization of the Armies of the United States.* New York and London: Thomas Yoseloff Publisher, 1959

Evans, Clement A. ed. *Confederate Military History.* Atlanta: Confederate Publishing Company, 1899. 12 vols.

Farrar, Samuel Clarke. *The Twenty Second Pennsylvania Cavalry and the Ringgold Battalion.* Pittsburgh, Pa.: Twenty Second Pennsylvania Ringgold Cavalry Association, 1911

Frye, Dennis E. *2nd Virginia Infantry*. H. E. Howard 1982

Gerties, Louis S. *The Civil War in Missouri: A Military History*. University of Missouri Press, 2012

Gottfried, Bradley M. *The Maps of Bull Run*. New York: Savas Beattie LLC, 2009

Hannings, Budd. *Every Day of the Civil War: A Chronological History*. McFarland, 2010

Harsh, Joseph L. *Sounding the Shallows: A Confederate Companion for the Maryland Campaign of 1862*. Kent State University Press, 2000

Hathaway, Seymour J. *History of Marietta and Washington County, Ohio, and Representative Citizens, Volume 1*. Biographical Publishing Company, 1902

Helm, Thomas B. *History of Cass County Indiana*. Brant and Fuller, 1886

Henderson, Lillian ed. *Roster of the Confederate soldiers of Georgia, 1861-1865*. Longino & Porter, 1960. 6 Vols

Hinze, David C. & Karen Farnham. *The Battle of Carthage: Border War in Southwest Missouri, July 5, 1861*. Savas Publishing Company, 1997

History of Lafayette County Missouri. Missouri Historical Company: St. Louis, 1881

Holcombe & Adams. *An Account of the Battle of Wilson's Creek*. Dow & Adams Publishers: Springfield Mo., 1883

Hughes, Nathaniel Cheairs. *The Battle of Belmont: Grant Strikes South*. University of North Carolina Press, 1991

Hunt, Roger D. *Colonels in Blue: Indiana, Kentucky, and Tennessee*. McFarland, 2014

Hunt, Roger D. *Colonels in Blue: New York*. Schiffer Publishing, 2003

Hunt, Roger D. *Colonels in Blue: Pennsylvania, New Jersey, Maryland, Delaware, and the District of Columbia*. Stackpole, 2007

Hunt, Roger D. *Colonels in Blue: The New England States*. Schiffer, 2001

Iobst, Richard W. *The Bloody Sixth: The Sixth North Carolina Regiment Confederate States of America*. Raleigh: North Carolina Confederate Centennial Commission, 1965

Jensen, Lee. *The 32nd Virginia* Infantry. H.E. Howard, 1990

Johnson, Robert U. and Clarence C. Buel, eds, *Battles and Leaders of the Civil War*. New York, 1887-88. 4 Vols.

Johnston, Joseph E. *Narrative of Military Operations Directed During the Late War Between the States*. New York: D. Appelton and Company, 1874

Knapp, Maj. George E. U.S. Army Retired. *The Wilson's Creek Staff Ride and Battlefield Tour*. Combat Studies Institute U.S. Army Command and General Staff College: Fort Leavenworth Kansas, 1993

Lindsley, John Berrien Ed. *The Military Annals of Tennessee: Confederate*. Nashville: J.M. Lindsley and Company Publishers, 1866

Lowry, Terry. *September Blood: The Battle of Carnifex Ferry*. Charleston, W.Va.: Pictorial Histories Publishing Company, 1988

Lowry, Terry. *The Battle of Scary Creek: Military Operations in the Kanawha Valley April-July 1861*. Charleston, W.Va.: Quarrier Press, 1998

Martin, George Winston. *"I Will Give Them One More Shot": Ramsey's 1st Regiment Georgia Volunteers*. Mercer University Press, 2005

Massachusetts Soldiers, Sailors, and Marines in the Civil War. Norwood Press, 1931. 8 Vols.

Maxwell, Jerry H. *The Perfect Lion, The Life and Death of Confederate Artillerist John Pelham*. Tuscaloosa: University of Alabama Press, 2011

Missouri Historical Review, Volume 1, Issues 2-4. State Historical Society of Missouri, 1907

Moore, Frank ed. *The Portrait Gallery of the War Civil, Military and Naval: A Biographical Record*. New York: D. Van Nostrand Publisher, 1865

Morton, Oren Frederic. *A History of Rockbridge County Virginia*. McClure Company, 1920

Oates, Stephen B. *Confederate Cavalry, West of the River*. University of Texas Press, 2010

Officers of the Continental and U.S. Navy and Marine Corps 1775-1900, "Navy Officers 1798-1900, L," *Naval History and Heritage Command*. Accessed February 26, 2014. http://www.history.navy.mil/browse-by-topic/organization-and-administration/historical-leadership/navy-and-marine-corps-officers-1775-1900.html

Officers of the Continental and U.S. Navy and Marine Corps 1775-1900, "Navy Officers 1798-1900, S," *Naval History and Heritage Command*. Accessed February 26, 2014. http://www.history.navy.mil/browse-by-topic/organization-and-administration/historical-leadership/navy-and-marine-corps-officers-1775-1900.html

Officers of the Continental and U.S. Navy and Marine Corps 1775-1900, "Navy Officers 1798-1900, R," *Naval History and Heritage Command*. Accessed February 26, 2014.

http://www.history.navy.mil/browse-by-topic/organization-and-administration/historical-leadership/navy-and-marine-corps-officers-1775-1900.html

Officers of the Continental and U.S. Navy and Marine Corps 1775-1900, "Navy Officers 1798-1900, W," *Naval History and Heritage Command.* Accessed February 26, 2014. http://www.history.navy.mil/browse-by-topic/organization-and-administration/historical-leadership/navy-and-marine-corps-officers-1775-1900.html

Officers of the Continental and U.S. Navy and Marine Corps 1775-1900, "Navy Officers 1798-1900, G," *Naval History and Heritage Command.* Accessed February 26, 2014. http://www.history.navy.mil/browse-by-topic/organization-and-administration/historical-leadership/navy-and-marine-corps-officers-1775-1900.html

Officers of the Continental and U.S. Navy and Marine Corps 1775-1900, "Navy Officers 1798-1900, N," *Naval History and Heritage Command.* Accessed February 26, 2014. http://www.history.navy.mil/browse-by-topic/organization-and-administration/historical-leadership/navy-and-marine-corps-officers-1775-1900.html

Officers of the Continental and U.S. Navy and Marine Corps 1775-1900, "Navy Officers 1798-1900, H," *Naval History and Heritage Command.* Accessed February 26, 2014. http://www.history.navy.mil/browse-by-topic/organization-and-administration/historical-leadership/navy-and-marine-corps-officers-1775-1900.html

Officers of the Continental and U.S. Navy and Marine Corps 1775-1900, "Navy Officers 1798-1900, K," *Naval History and Heritage Command.* Accessed February 26, 2014. http://www.history.navy.mil/browse-by-topic/organization-and-administration/historical-leadership/navy-and-marine-corps-officers-1775-1900.html

Official Army Register for September 1861, Adjutant Generals Office, 1861

Official Records of the Union and Confederate Navies in the War of the Rebellion. Government Printing Office: Washington D.C., 1894-1922. 30 Vols.

Official Roster of the Soldiers of the State of Ohio in the War of the Rebellion 1861-1866. The Werner Company: Akron, 1893. 12 Vols.

Peterson, Richard C. et al., *Sterling Price's Lieutenants: A Guide to the Officers and Organization of the Missouri State Guard 1861-1865 Revised Edition.* Independence, Mo.: Two Trails Publishing, 2007

Phisterer, Frederick. *New York in the War of the Rebellion 1861 to 1865.* J.B. Lyon Company, State Printer, 1912

Phisterer, Frederick. *Statistical Record of the Armies of the United States.* New York: Charles Scribner's Sons, 1883

Pinnell, Allen. *Serving with Honor: The Diary of Captain Eathan Allen Pinnell, Eighth Missouri Infantry (Confederate).* NP:ND

Piston, William Garrett & Richard W. Hatcher III, *Wilson's Creek: The Second Battle of the Civil War and the Men Who Fought It.* University of North Carolina Press, 2000

Poland, Charles Preston. *Glories of War: Small Battles and Early Heroes of 1861.* AuthorHouse, 2006

Radley, Kenneth J. *Rebel Watchdog The Confederate States Army Provost Guard.* LSU Press, 1989

Record of service of Michigan volunteers in the civil war, 1861-1865. Ihling Bros. & Everard, Printers, N.D. 46 Vols.

Records of officers and men of New Jersey in the Civil War, 1861-1865. Trenton: John L. Murphy Steam Book and Job Printer, 1876. 2 Vols.

Report of the Adjutant General of the State of Indiana 1861-1865, Indianapolis: W.B. Holloway State Printer, 1865. 8 Vols.

Revised Register of the Soldiers and Sailors of New Hampshire in the War of Rebellion 1861-1866. Concord: Ira C. Evans Public Printer, 1895

Rowland, Dunbar. *The Official and Statistical Record of the State of Mississippi 1908.* Nashville: Brandon Printing Company, 1908

Scott, Douglas D., Thomas D. Thiessen, and Steve J. Dasovich. *The "First" Battle of Boonville, Cooper County, Missouri, June 17, 1861: Archaeological and Historical Investigations.* Missouri Civil War Heritage Foundation, 2009

Scott, J. L. *36th and 37th Battalions Virginia Cavalry.* H.E. Howard, 1986

Seigler, Robert S. *South Carolina's Military Organizations During the War Between the States.* Charleston: The History Press, 2008. 4 Vols.

Sibley, F. Ray Jr. *Confederate Artillery Organizations: An Alphabetical Listing of the Officers and Batteries of the Confederacy 1861-1865.* Savas Beattie LLC, 2014

Sifakis, Stewart. *Compendium of the Confederate Armies.* New York: Facts on File Inc., 1992. 10 Vols.

Skoch, George and Mark W. Perkins. *Lone Star Confederate: A Gallant and Good Soldier of the Fifth Texas Infantry.* Texas A&M University Press, 2003

Smith, Derek. *The Gallant Dead: Union and Confederate Generals Killed in the Civil War.* Mechanicsburg Pennsylvania: Stackpole Books, 2008

Smith, Steven M. and Patrick Hook. *The Stonewall Brigade in the Civil War.* Minneapolis, Zenith Press, 2008

Speed, Captain Thomas et al., *The Union Regiments of Kentucky*, Louisville, Kentucky: Courier-Journal Job Printing Company, 1897

Stanley, Dick. "Captain Lorenzo Dow Fletcher," *13th Mississippi Infantry Regiment*, (July 11, 2015). Accessed December 22, 2015, http://13thmississippi.com/2015/07/11/captain-lorenzo-dow-fletcher/

The Battle of Lexington, Fought in and Around the City of Lexington, Missouri, on September 18th, 19th and 20th, 1861, by Forces Under Command of Colonel James A. Mulligan, and General Sterling Price. The Official Records of Both Parties to the Conflict; to which is Added Memoirs of Participants. Lexington Historical Society, 1903

The Union Army: A History of Military Affairs in the Loyal States 1861-65. Federal Publishing Company: Madison Wis., 1908. 8 Vols.

The War of the Rebellion: A Compilation of the Official Records of the Union and Confederate Armies. Washington D.C. 1880-1891. 128 Vols.

Thompson, Ilene D., Wilbur E. Thompson, *The Seventeenth Alabama: A Regimental History and Roster.* Heritage Books, 2001

Wallace, Lee A. Jr. *A Guide to Virginia Military Organizations 1861-1865.* H.E. Howard, Inc., 1986

Warner, Ezra J. *Generals in Gray.* Baton Rouge: Louisiana State University Press, 1987

Welcher, Frank J. *The Union Army 1861-1865 Organization and Operations Volume 1: The Eastern Theater.* Bloomington and Indianapolis: Indiana University Press, 1989

Welsh, Jack D. *Medical Histories of Confederate Generals*, Kent State University Press, 1999

Welsh, Jack D. *Medical Histories of Union Generals.* Kent State University Press, 2005

Whitman, William E.S. and Charles H. True. *Maine in the War for the Union.* Nelson Dingley Jr. & Co. Publishers, 1865

Wisconsin Adjutant General's Office, *Roster of Wisconsin Volunteers, War of the Rebellion, 1861-1865.* Madison: Democrat Printing Company, 1886. 2 Vols.

Wise, Jennings Cropper. *The Long Arm of Lee or History of the Artillery of the Army of Northern Virginia.* Lynchburg, Va.: J.P. Bell & Company, 1915

Wood, Larry. *The Siege of Lexington Missouri: The Battle of the Hemp Bales.* The History Press, 2014

Worsham, John H. *One of Jackson's Foot Cavalry.* The Neale Publishing Company, 1912

Wyllie, Arthur. *Confederate Officers.* N.P., 2007

Zinn, Jack *R.E. Lee's Cheat Mountain Campaign.* McClain Print Co., 1974

Index

1

100th Pennsylvania 59
10th Alabama 27, 67
10th Arkansas 58
10th Indiana 15
10th Mississippi 51, 64
10th Ohio 37
10th Pennsylvania 21
10th Pennsylvania Reserves 67
10th Virginia 27
114th Virginia Militia 48
119th Virginia Militia 9
11th Alabama 27
11th Georgia 26
11th Indiana 23
11th Louisiana 57
11th Massachusetts 19
11th Mississippi 26
11th Missouri 52
11th New York 20
11th North Carolina 23
11th Ohio 8
11th Pennsylvania 22
11th Tennessee 55
11th Virginia 24, 67
120th Virginia Militia 9
126th Virginia Militia 9
129th Virginia Militia 9
12th Georgia 41, 50, 65
12th Louisiana 58
12th New York 18, 22
12th Ohio 8, 37
12th Ohio Independent Battery 39
12th Pennsylvania Reserves 67
12th South Carolina 61
12th Tennessee 56
13th Arkansas 57
13th Indiana 15, 39, 49, 65
13th Mississippi 24, 54, 77
13th Missouri 43
13th New York 18
13th Ohio 16, 37
13th Pennsylvania 22
13th Tennessee 56
13th Virginia 27
142nd Virginia Militia 9
14th Georgia 40
14th Indiana 15, 39, 49
14th Missouri Home Guard 43
14th New York (Militia) 19
14th Ohio 10, 15, 55
14th Pennsylvania 22
14th Tennessee 40
14th Virginia Cavalry 16
154th Senior Tennessee 57
15th Illinois Cavalry 56
15th Indiana 15, 39, 49
15th Massachusetts 54
15th Mississippi 55
15th New York 21
15th Ohio 10, 16
15th Pennsylvania 22
15th South Carolina 61
15th Tennessee 56
16th New York 21
16th Ohio 10, 16
16th Pennsylvania 22
16th Tennessee 40
17th Alabama 64
17th Illinois 52
17th Indiana 39, 49
17th Mississippi 23, 54
17th Ohio 15, 55
17th Pennsylvania 22
17th South Carolina State Militia 6
17th Tennessee 55
17th Virginia 24
184th Virginia Militia 9
187th Virginia Militia 9
18th Mississippi 23, 54
18th New York 21
18th Ohio 16
18th Virginia 24
190th Virginia Militia 9
19th Indiana 42
19th Mississippi 27
19th New York 22
19th Ohio 15
19th Tennessee 55
19th Virginia 24
1st (Price's Rifles) Missouri State Guard Light Artillery Battery (8th) 14, 32, 36, 46
1st Alabama 51, 64
1st Arkansas 24, 30, 66
1st Arkansas Mounted Rifles 30
1st Battalion Confederate States Provisional Army 40
1st Connecticut 18
1st Florida 51, 64
1st Georgia 17, 41, 50
1st Georgia Battalion 64
1st Illinois Artillery (B) 52
1st Illinois Cavalry 43

1st Illinois Light Artillery (B) 56
1st Indiana Cavalry 52
1st Iowa 29
1st Kansas 29
1st Kansas Light Artillery 35
1st Kentucky (CS) 67
1st Kentucky (U.S.) 8
1st Kentucky Battalion 26
1st Kentucky Cavalry (US) 55
1st Kentucky Cavalry Battalion (CS) 62
1st Kentucky Independent Battery 8
1st Louisiana 64
1st Louisiana Battalion 24
1st Maryland 27
1st Massachusetts 18
1st Michigan 20
1st Michigan Artillery (A) 39, 49
1st Michigan Light Artillery (A) 15
1st Minnesota 19
1st Mississippi Battalion 57
1st Mississippi Cavalry Battalion 57
1st Missouri 58
1st Missouri (U.S.) 12, 29
1st Missouri Light Artillery Battery 52
1st Missouri State Guard (1st) 52
1st Missouri State Guard (2nd) 43
1st Missouri State Guard (3rd) 13, 30, 35, 44
1st Missouri State Guard (4th) 13, 31, 35, 44
1st Missouri State Guard (5th) 44, 47
1st Missouri State Guard (6th) 13, 31, 45
1st Missouri State Guard (7th) 31, 45
1st Missouri State Guard (8th) 14, 31, 36, 45
1st Missouri State Guard (Platte County) Battalion (5th) .45, 47
1st Missouri State Guard Battalion (1st) 52
1st Missouri State Guard Battalion (2nd) 43
1st Missouri State Guard Battalion (3rd) 35, 44
1st Missouri State Guard Battalion (4th) 31
1st Missouri State Guard Battalion (5th) 45, 47
1st Missouri State Guard Cavalry (1st) 53
1st Missouri State Guard Cavalry (2nd) 43
1st Missouri State Guard Cavalry (4th) 13, 31, 35, 44
1st Missouri State Guard Cavalry (6th) 13, 31, 45
1st Missouri State Guard Cavalry (8th) 14, 32, 36, 46
1st Missouri State Guard Cavalry Battalion (2nd) 44
1st Missouri State Guard Cavalry Battalion (3rd)..13, 30, 44
1st Missouri State Guard Cavalry Battalion (4th) 13
1st Missouri State Guard Cavalry Battalion (5th) 35, 45
1st Missouri State Guard Cavalry Battalion (E) (7th).31, 36, 45
1st Missouri State Guard Light Artillery Battery (6th)13, 31, 35, 45
1st Missouri State Guard Rifles 12
1st New Hampshire 22
1st New Jersey 20
1st New Jersey (Militia) 20
1st New York 11
1st New York Engineers 59
1st North Carolina 11
1st North Carolina Artillery (F) 34
1st North Carolina Cavalry 67
1st Ohio 18
1st Ohio Cavalry 15, 39, 49
1st Ohio Independent Battery 37
1st Ohio Light Artillery (A) 15
1st Ohio Light Artillery (B) 15, 55
1st Ohio Light Artillery (C) 15
1st Ohio Light Artillery (D) 10, 16
1st Ohio Light Artillery (E) 16
1st Ohio Light Artillery (F) 10, 16
1st Pennsylvania 22
1st Pennsylvania Cavalry 67
1st Pennsylvania Reserve Rifles 67
1st Pennsylvania Reserves Light Artillery (A) 67
1st Rhode Island 19
1st Rhode Island Artillery (A) 23
1st Rhode Island Artillery (B) 54
1st South Carolina 6, 7, 23
1st South Carolina Militia Artillery 61
1st South Carolina Provisional Army 6
1st South Carolina Regulars 7
1st South Carolina State Militia Rifles 7
1st Tennessee 40
1st Tennessee Cavalry Battalion 55
1st Tennessee Provisional Army 27
1st United States Artillery (A) 51, 63
1st United States Artillery (E) 6, 21
1st United States Artillery (F) 63
1st United States Artillery (G) 19
1st United States Artillery (H) 6
1st United States Artillery (I) 20, 54
1st United States Artillery (L) 63
1st United States Cavalry (B) 29
1st United States Cavalry (I) 30
1st United States Chasseurs 42
1st Vermont 11
1st Virginia 24, 40
1st Virginia Cavalry 28
1st Virginia Cavalry (Company E [Valley Rangers]) 42
1st West Virginia 10
1st West Virginia Artillery (A) 40, 49
1st West Virginia Cavalry 37
1st West Virginia Light Artillery (A) 16
1st Wisconsin 22

2

20th Illinois 52
20th Massachusetts 54
20th New York 34

Unit	Pages
20th Ohio	16
20th Pennsylvania (Scott Legion)	21
20th Tennessee	55
20th Virginia	16
21st Illinois	52
21st Ohio	8, 62
21st Pennsylvania	21
21st Tennessee	56
21st Virginia	40
22nd Illinois	56
22nd Mississippi	58
22nd Ohio	16
22nd Tennessee	56
22nd Virginia	8, 33, 37
23rd Illinois	43
23rd Ohio	37
23rd Pennsylvania	21
23rd Virginia	17, 41, 50
24th Ohio	39, 49
24th Pennsylvania	22
24th Virginia	24
25th Mississippi	58
25th New York	21
25th Ohio	39, 49, 65
25th Pennsylvania	22
25th Virginia	16, 41, 50, 65
26th New York	21
27th Illinois	56
27th Missouri Mounted Infantry	43
27th New York	19
27th Pennsylvania	21
27th Virginia	26
28th New York	23
28th Ohio	37
28th Virginia	24
29th New York	21
2nd (3rd) Tennessee Cavalry Battalion	55
2nd (Palmetto Regiment) South Carolina	6
2nd and 3rd United States	22
2nd Arkansas	66
2nd Arkansas Mounted Rifles	30
2nd Connecticut	18
2nd Kansas	29
2nd Kentucky (U.S.)	8
2nd Maine	18
2nd Massachusetts	22
2nd Michigan	18
2nd Mississippi	26
2nd Missouri (U.S.)	12, 29
2nd Missouri State Guard (1st)	52
2nd Missouri State Guard (3rd)	44
2nd Missouri State Guard (4th)	44, 47
2nd Missouri State Guard (6th)	35, 45
2nd Missouri State Guard (7th)	31, 36, 45
2nd Missouri State Guard (8th)	14, 31, 36, 45
2nd Missouri State Guard Battalion (1st)	53
2nd Missouri State Guard Battalion (2nd)	43
2nd Missouri State Guard Battalion (3rd)	35, 44
2nd Missouri State Guard Cavalry (1st)	53
2nd Missouri State Guard Cavalry (2nd)	44
2nd Missouri State Guard Cavalry (5th)	45, 47
2nd Missouri State Guard Cavalry (6th)	45
2nd Missouri State Guard Cavalry (8th)	14, 32, 36, 46
2nd New Hampshire	19
2nd New Jersey	20
2nd New Jersey (Militia)	20
2nd New York	11, 18
2nd Ohio	18, 62
2nd Pennsylvania	22
2nd Rhode Island	19
2nd Rhode Island Battery	19
2nd South Carolina	23
2nd Tennessee	24, 56
2nd U.S. Artillery (C)	63
2nd United States	12
2nd United States Artillery	63
2nd United States Artillery (A)	21
2nd United States Artillery (B)	11
2nd United States Artillery (C)	63
2nd United States Artillery (D)	20
2nd United States Artillery (E)	18
2nd United States Artillery (F)	12, 29
2nd United States Artillery (G)	21
2nd United States Artillery (H)	51, 63
2nd United States Artillery (K)	63
2nd United States Artillery (M)	19
2nd United States Artillery (Section)	34
2nd United States Dragoons (C)	30
2nd Vermont	20, 42
2nd Virginia	24, 25, 71
2nd Virginia Cavalry	67
2nd Virginia Cavalry (Company A [Clay Dragoons])	24
2nd Virginia Cavalry (Company I [Campbell Rangers])	24
2nd West Virginia	39, 65
2nd Wisconsin	18

3

Unit	Pages
30th Illinois	56
30th Ohio	37
30th Virginia Cavalry	25
31st Illinois	56
31st New York	21
31st Virginia	17, 41, 49, 65
32nd Indiana	66
32nd New York	21
32nd Ohio	39, 49, 65
33rd Illinois	52
33rd Indiana	55
33rd Ohio	62

33rd Virginia 26
36th Virginia 9, 33, 38
37th New York 21
37th Virginia 17, 41, 50
38th Illinois 52
38th New York 20
38th Virginia 27
39th New York 21
3rd Arkansas 30, 41, 49
3rd Arkansas Battalion 30
3rd Connecticut 18
3rd Iowa 47
3rd Kansas 35
3rd Louisiana 30
3rd Maine 20
3rd Michigan 19
3rd Missouri (U.S.) 13, 29
3rd Missouri State Guard (1st) 52
3rd Missouri State Guard (5th) 45
3rd Missouri State Guard (8th) 14, 31, 36, 46
3rd Missouri State Guard Battalion (1st) 53
3rd Missouri State Guard Cavalry (1st) 53
3rd Missouri State Guard Cavalry (2nd) 44
3rd Missouri State Guard Cavalry (6th) 45
3rd Missouri State Guard Cavalry (8th) 14, 32, 36, 46
3rd New Hampshire 59
3rd New Jersey 20
3rd New Jersey (Militia) 20
3rd New York 11
3rd New York (G) 51
3rd New York Battery 42
3rd Ohio 15, 39
3rd Pennsylvania 22
3rd Rhode Island 59
3rd South Carolina 23
3rd Tennessee Provisional Army 27
3rd United States (C) 51, 63
3rd United States (E) 51, 63
3rd United States Artillery (E) 18, 59
3rd Vermont 42
3rd Virginia 11
3rd Virginia Cavalry 11
3rd West Virginia 39
3rd Wisconsin 23

4
41st New York 20
42nd New York 54
42nd Virginia 40
44th Virginia 16, 41, 50
45th Virginia 33, 38
46th New York 59
47th New York 59
47th Ohio 37
48th New York 59

48th Virginia 40
49th Virginia 24
4th Alabama 26
4th Arkansas 30
4th Connecticut 22
4th Georgia Battalion 60
4th Kansas 35
4th Maine 20
4th Massachusetts 11
4th Michigan 20
4th Missouri State Guard (1st) 52
4th Missouri State Guard Battalion (8th) 14, 31, 36, 46
4th Missouri State Guard Cavalry (2nd) 44
4th Missouri State Guard Cavalry (8th) 14, 32, 36, 46
4th New Hampshire 59
4th New Jersey (Militia) 20
4th Ohio 15, 48
4th Pennsylvania 20
4th South Carolina 24
4th Tennessee 58
4th United States Artillery (F) 23
4th United States Artillery (G) 16, 39, 49
4th United States Artillery (I) 16, 37
4th Virginia 25
4th Virginia Cavalry (Company A [Prince William Cavalry]) 25
4th Virginia Cavalry (Company B [Chesterfield Light Dragoons]) 25
4th Virginia Cavalry (Company D [Little Fork Rangers]) 25
4th Virginia Cavalry (Company E [Powhatan Troop]) 25
4th Virginia Cavalry (Company F [Goochland Light Dragoons]) 25
4th Virginia Cavalry (Company G [Hanover Light Dragoons]) 25
4th Virginia Cavalry (Company H [Black Horse Troop]) . 25
4th Virginia Cavalry (Company I [Governor's Mounted Guard]) 25
4th Wisconsin 23

5
50th Pennsylvania 59
50th Virginia 33, 38
51st Virginia 33, 38
52nd Virginia 41, 49, 65
59th Ohio 62
59th Virginia 9, 33, 38
5th Alabama 23
5th Arkansas 30
5th Georgia 51, 64
5th Kansas Cavalry 35
5th Kentucky (CS) 62
5th Louisiana Battalion 57
5th Maine 20
5th Massachusetts 19
5th Missouri (U.S.) 13, 30

5th Missouri State Guard (8th) 14, 31, 36, 46
5th Missouri State Guard Cavalry (8th) 14, 32, 36, 46
5th New York 11, 22
5th North Carolina 24
5th Ohio 16
5th South Carolina 23
5th Tennessee 57
5th United States Artillery (D) 19, 42
5th United States Cavalry 19
5th United States Cavalry (H) 42
5th Virginia 26

6
69th New York 18
6th (16th) North Carolina 40
6th Alabama 23
6th Connecticut 59
6th Indiana 10, 15
6th Kansas Cavalry 35
6th Louisiana 23
6th Missouri State Guard Cavalry (8th) 14, 32, 36, 46
6th New York (D) 63
6th New York (G) 63
6th New York (H) 63
6th New York (I) 63
6th New York (K) 63
6th North Carolina 27
6th Ohio 15, 39
6th Pennsylvania 21
6th Pennsylvania Reserves 67
6th South Carolina 67
6th Tennessee 57
6th Tennessee Cavalry Battalion 57

7
71st New York 19
71st Pennsylvania 54
77th Virginia Militia 48
79th New York 18, 42, 59
7th Alabama 51
7th Connecticut 59
7th Georgia 26
7th Indiana 10, 15, 39, 49
7th Iowa 56
7th Kansas Cavalry 35
7th Kentucky (US) 55
7th Louisiana 24
7th Missouri State Guard Cavalry (8th) 14, 32, 36
7th New York 11
7th North Carolina 34
7th Ohio 15, 33
7th Pennsylvania 21
7th South Carolina 23
7th Tennessee 40
7th Virginia 24
7th Virginia Cavalry 48

8
83rd New York 22
8th Alabama 27
8th Georgia 26
8th Indiana 15
8th Louisiana 23
8th Maine 59
8th Michigan 59
8th New York 21
8th New York (Militia) 19
8th New York Militia Battery 21
8th Ohio 16, 48
8th Pennsylvania 21
8th South Carolina 23
8th Tennessee 40
8th Texas Cavalry (1st Texas Rangers) 66
8th Virginia 24, 54
8th Wisconsin 52

9
9th [11th] South Carolina 60, 61
9th Alabama 27
9th Arkansas 57
9th Georgia 26
9th Indiana 10, 15, 39, 49, 65
9th Maine 59
9th Mississippi 64
9th Missouri State Guard Cavalry (8th) 14
9th Missouri State Guard Cavalry Battalion (8th) 36
9th New York 34, 51
9th Ohio 15, 37
9th Pennsylvania 22
9th Pennsylvania Reserves 67
9th Tennessee 57
9th Virginia Battalion 17, 41, 49, 65
9th Virginia Cavalry 40

A
Abercrombie, John J. 22
Adams, _ 43
Adams, Daniel W. 64
Adams, Stephen A. 33, 38
Albert, Anselm 29
Alburtis, Ephraim G. 26
Alexander, Charles B. 45
Alexander, John D. 24
Alexander, John W. S. 52
Alexander, W. 40
Allen, Harvey A. 63
Allen, James W. 25
Allen, William H. 11
Ammen, Daniel 60
Ammen, Jacob 39, 49
Anderson, George T. 26
Anderson, James Patton 51, 64
Anderson, Pierce B. 17, 41, 50, 65

Anderson, Richard H. 7, 51, 64
Anderson, Robert 6
Anderson, Samuel R. 40
Andrews, George L. 29
Andrews, George W. 16
Andrews, Lorin 15
Andrews, William S. G. 34
Apperson, Richard 62
Arkansas (Reid's [Fort Smith Battery]) Battery 30
Arkansas (Woodruff's) Battery 30
Arnold, Lewis G. 51, 63
Arnold, Richard 20
Atchison, David R. 47
Atkins, John D. 57
Austin, Andrew J. 31
Ayres, Romeyn B. 18

B
Backof, Franz 13, 29
Bacon, Thomas G. 23
Bailey, Robert 63
Baker, Conrad 52
Baker, Edward D. 54
Baker, Henry M. 20
Balch, Joseph P. 19
Baldwin, John F. 41, 49
Ball, William B. 25
Ballier, John F. 21
Bankhead, John P. 60
Bankhead, Smith P. 57
Barksdale, William 24
Barlow, William P. 31
Barnett, James 15
Barron, Samuel 34
Barrow, Robert H. 57
Bartlett, Joseph J. 19
Barton, Seth M. 41, 49
Bartow, Francis S. 26
Batchelor, S. S. 64
Bate, William B. 24
Bates, John F. 29
Battle, Joel A. 55
Baughan, Richard A. 14
Beatty, Samuel 15
Beaufort (South Carolina) Guerillas 61
Beauregard, Pierre G. T. 6, 23
Becker, Frederick 43
Beckett, Albert J. 33, 38
Beckham, Robert F. 27
Beckley, Alfred 9
Bee, Barnard E. 26
Bell, Tyree H. 56
Beltzhoover, Daniel M. 58
Bendix, John E. 11
Benham, Henry W. 37

Benton, William P. 15
Berry, Hiram G. 20
Bevier, Robert S. 35, 44
Bickerton, Thomas 35
Bidwell, Alonzo F. 20
Birthright, Claiborne E. 52
Bischoff, Henry 13
Blair Jr., Francis P. Blair 12
Blair, Charles W. 29
Blanton, William C. 44
Bledsoe, Hiram M. 14, 32, 36, 46
Blenker, Louis 20
Blunt, Matthew M. 63
Blythe, Andrew K. 57
Bohannon, Louis C. 31, 35, 44
Bonham, DeWitt C. 58
Bonham, Milledge L. 23
Bookwood, Charles 21
Border Guards 33, 38
Border Rangers (Company E, 8th Virginia Cavalry)... 33, 38
Bosley, William K. 15, 39
Bowen, John S. 58
Bowie, Alexander W. 58
Boyd, John R. 45, 47
Boykin Jr., Francis M. 65
Brace, Theodore 44
Bracken, James R. 39, 49
Bradley, John M. 57
Bragg, Braxton 64
Bramhall, Walter M. 54
Brashear, Ezra J. 31
Brazelton Jr., William N. 55
Brown, Harvey 51, 63
Brown, John Thompson 11
Brown, Nathaniel W. 59
Brown, Thomas 52
Brown, William B. 13, 31
Brumby, Arnoldus V. 40
Budd, Thomas A. 60
Buford, Napoleon B. 56
Burbridge, John Q. 13, 30
Burke, John 21
Burks, Jesse S. 40
Burnham, George S. 18
Burnside, Ambrose E. 19
Bursdal, Henry W. 15
Burt, Erasmus R. 23, 54
Butler, Benjamin F. 34
Butler, William 7
Butterfield, Daniel 22

C
C.S.S. Resolute 61
C.S.S. Sampson 61
C.S.S. Savannah 61

Cabell County Border Rangers 9
Cabell, John G. 25
Cadwalader, George 21
Cake, Henry L. 22
Caldwell, Joseph 9
Calhoun, William R. 7
Camden Jr., Gideon D. 65
Cameron, James 18
Campbell, Edward 9
Campbell, John A. 40
Campbell, Leonidas St. Clair 31, 36, 45
Canfield, Charles W. 29
Carlin, William P. 52
Carlisle, John Howard 18
Carlton, Henry H. 40
Carnes, William W. 56
Carr, Eugene A. 30
Carr, Joseph B. 11
Carroll, Charles A. 30
Carroll, Charles M. 56
Carroll, DeRossy 30
Cash, Ellerbee B. C. 23
Catlin, James K. 56
Cawthorn, James 14, 31
Chalfin, Samuel F. 63
Chalmers, A. H. 44
Chalmers, James R. 51, 64
Champion, John R. 45
Charleston Light Dragoons 7
Chatfield, John L. 18, 59
Chauncey, John S. 34
Cheatham, Benjamin F. 57
Chicago Dragoons 37
Childs, Richard 44, 47
Christ, Benjamin C. 59
Christian, Samuel P. 66
Christian, William H. 21
Churchill, Thomas J. 30
Clark Jr., George 19
Clark Jr., John B. 30, 35, 44
Clark Sr., John B. 13, 30
Clark, Samuel Churchill 46
Clark's Light Artillery Battery 46
Clarke, John S. 22
Clarkson, James J. 14, 31, 36, 46
Clayton, Henry D. 64
Closson, Henry W. 63
Coburn, John 55
Cocke, Philip St. George 24
Coffee, John T. 46
Cogswell, Milton 54
Cole, Warren 58
Collins, Napoleon 60
Connell, John M. 15, 55

Conner, James 25
Conner, Zephaniah T. 50, 65
Cooper, Thomas L. 26
Corcoran, Michael 18
Cordes, Theodore 7
Corns, James M. 9, 33, 38
Corse, Montgomery D. 24
Cotter, Charles S. 8
Cowdin, Robert 18
Cox, Jacob D. 8
Cravens, Jeremiah C. 14, 32, 36, 46
Crittenden, Thomas T. 10, 15
Crosby, Pierce 34
Cummings, Arthur C. 26
Cummings, David H. 55
Cummings, Thomas B. 14, 36
Cundiff, James H. R. 45
Cunningham, John 6
Cuthbert, George B. 6
Cutts, Allen S. 67
D
D'Utassy, Frederick G. 21
Dabney, Chiswell E. 65
Dare, Charles P. 21
Daum, Philip 16, 40, 49
Davidson, George S. 24
Davies, Thomas A. 21
Davis, Charles H. 59
De Jernatt, John 9
Deitzler, George W. 29
DeLagnel, Julius A. 16
Depuy, Herman G. 16, 48
DeSaussure, Wilmot G. 6, 61
Devens Jr., Charles 54
DeVilliers, Charles 8
Dickey, Moses R. 10
Dills, George K. 35, 45
Dobie, James H. 51, 63
Dockery, Thomas P. 30
Dollins, James J. 56
Donelson, Daniel S. 40
Donnelly, Dudley 23
Doubleday, Abner 6, 21
Dougherty, Henry 56
Douglass, Henry L. 57
Drayton, Percival 59
Drayton, Thomas F. 60
Dubois, John V. 29
Duffy, Patrick 63
Dumont, Ebenezer 10, 15
Duncan, Blanton 26
Dunnell, Mark H. 20
Dunning, Samuel H. 16
Dunovant, John 7

Dunovant, Richard G. M. 61
DuPont, Samuel H. 59
Duryea, Abram 11
Duryea, Richard C. 63

E
Early, Jubal A. 24
Easton, Hezekiah 67
Echols, John 26
Edmonds, Edward C. 27
Edwards, John 19
Einstein, Max 21
Elliott Jr., Stephen 61
Elliott, Benjamin F. 45
Elliott, Samuel M. 18
Ellison, Francis B. 63
Elzey, Arnold 27
Embry, Benjamin T. 30
Emley, Anthony H. 21
Enyart, David A. 8
Eshelman, Benjamin F. 25
Essig, Christian 13
Evans, Nathan G. 7, 24, 54
Ewell, Richard S. 23
Ewing, Hugh B. 37

F
Fagan, James F. 24
Falkner, William C. 26
Farmer, Benjamin J. 52
Farnsworth, Addison 20
Farrend, Charles E. 30
Faulkner, Jefferson L. 58
Fayette Rangers 9
Featherston, Winfield S. 23, 54
Fellows, Enoch Q. 59
Fenton, William M. 59
Fisher, Charles F. 27
Fiske, Frank S. 19
Fitzpatrick, Thomas P. 33, 38
Fletcher, Lorenzo D. 54
Floyd, John B. 33, 37
Forbes, John H. 31
Forbes, William A. 40
Ford, Thomas H. 39, 49, 65
Forney, John H. 27, 67
Foster, John A. 31
Foster, John G. 6
Fouke, Philip B. 56
Fowler, Edward B. 19
Franklin, William B. 19
Freedom Township Company 43
Freeman, Thomas J. 56
French, Frank S. 54
Frizell, Joseph W. 8
Fulkerson, Samuel V. 17, 41, 50

Fulton, Alfred S. 40
Funsten, Oliver R. 48
Fyffe, James P. 62

G
Gardner, William M. 26
Garland Jr., Samuel 24, 67
Garnett, Robert S. 16, 17
Garrard, Theophilus T. 55
Gartrell, Lucius J. 26
Gavin, James 39, 49
George, John S. 8
Georgia (Read's) Battery 61
Georgia (Sumter Flying Artillery) Battery 67
Georgia (Troup Artillery) Battery 40
German Hussars 7
Gibbes, Wade H. 7
Gibbons, Simeon B. 27
Gilham, William 40
Gillis, John P. 34, 60
Gilmore, George L. 37
Gist, States Rights 26
Gladden, Adley H. 64
Gordon, George H. 22
Gordon, James B. 67
Gordon, Sylvanus W. 59
Gorman, Willis A. 19
Goulding, Edwin R. 26
Govan, Daniel C. 66
Grant, Ulysses S. 56
Gratiot, John R. 30
Graves, John R. 14, 31, 36
Gray, William H. 21
Greble, John T. 11
Green, Martin E. 43
Greenbrier Cavalry Company 40
Greene, Oliver D. 21
Greer, Elkanah 30
Gregg, Maxcy 6, 23
Griffin, Charles 19, 42
Griffin, Thomas M. 54
Griffin, William 12
Grover, Benjamin W. 43
Groves, George A. 27
Guibor, Henry C. 13, 31, 35, 45
Guthrie, James V. 8
Guy, John H. 33, 38

H
Haggerty, Francis S. 60
Hagood, Johnson 6
Hairston, Peter 24
Halderman, John A. 29
Hale, John P. 9
Hallonquist, James H. 7, 51
Hamilton, Charles S. 23

Hamilton, John	59
Hamilton, John R.	7
Hamilton, S. H. D.	57
Hampton (South Carolina) Legion	24
Hampton, Wade	24
Hangen, William H. H.	22
Hansard, Calvin B.	44
Hansbrough, George W.	17, 41, 65
Harper, Kenton	26
Harris, Leonard A.	62
Harris, Robert A.	24
Harris, Samuel S.	53
Harris, Thomas A.	43
Harrison, George F.	25
Harrison, John J.	61
Harrison, Julian	25
Hart, Harrison E.	56
Hartranft, John F.	20
Haskell, Milo S.	39, 49
Hassendeubel, Francis	13
Hatton, Robert	40
Hawkins, Henry P.	52
Hawkins, Rush C.	34
Hays, Harry T.	24
Haywood, Robert	58
Hebert, Louis	30
Heck, Jonathan M.	16, 41
Heckman, Louis	16
Hedgepeth, Isaac N.	52
Heintzelman, Samuel P.	19
Henderson, William N.	9
Heth, Henry	33, 38
Heuberer, Charles E.	63
Hewes, David T.	39
Heyward, William C.	60
Higginbotham, John C.	50
Higgins, Jacob C.	67
Hildt, John M.	51, 63
Hill, Ambrose Powell	27
Hill, Charles W.	16
Hill, Daniel Harvey	11
Hindman, Thomas C.	66
Holmes, Theophilus H.	24
Homer's Artillery Company	51
Hood, John Bell	11
Houston, Arch	29
Hovey, Charles E.	52
Howard, Oliver O.	20
Howe, Albion P.	16, 39, 49
Hudson, Alfred	57
Hudson, Clement L.	58
Huger, Arthur M.	61
Huger, Cleland K.	7
Hughes, John T.	13, 31, 35, 44
Hull Jr., Edward B.	44
Humes, William Y. C.	58
Hunt, Henry J.	19
Hunter, David	19
Hunter, DeWitt C.	32, 36
Hunton, Eppa	24, 54
Hurst, Edgar V. R.	14, 31, 36, 46
Hyde, Breed N.	42

I

Illinois Cavalry Company	52
Imboden, John D.	27
Independent Missouri State Guard Cavalry Company (1st)	53
Irvine, John	10, 16
Irwin, William H.	21
Isaacson, Harry M.	25

J

Jackson Jr., Andrew	58
Jackson, Claiborne F.	13
Jackson, Congreve	44
Jackson, Conrad Feger	67
Jackson, George	17, 41, 50
Jackson, Henry R.	40, 49
Jackson, John K.	51, 64
Jackson, Richard H.	63
Jackson, Thomas E.	33, 38
Jackson, Thomas J.	25
Jackson, William A.	21
Jackson, William H.	56
Jackson, William L.	17, 41, 49
James, George S.	7
Jameson, Charles D.	18
Jarrett, Phaon	22
Jenifer, Walter H.	25, 54
Jenkins, Albert G.	9
Jenkins, Micah	23
Jenkins, William K.	10
Jennings, Daniel	53
Jennison, Charles R.	35
Johnson, Aaron C.	39
Johnson, Adolphus J.	20
Johnson, Edward	41, 50, 65
Johnson, Hampton P.	35
Johnson, James M.	45
Johnston, John W.	22
Johnston, Joseph E.	25, 26
Jones, David R.	23
Jones, Egbert J.	26
Jones, J. Pembroke	61
Jones, John A.	39, 49, 65
Jones, Joseph P.	24
Jones, Samuel	25
Jones, Timothy P.	57
Judson, William R.	35

K

- Kanawha Rangers 9
- Kane, Thomas L. 67
- Keim, William H. 22
- Kelly, Benjamin F. 10
- Kelly, Ephriam V. 45
- Kelly, Henry B. 23
- Kelly, James 18
- Kelly, Joseph 13, 31
- Kelly's (Irish) Light Artillery Battery 45
- Kemble, William F. 9
- Kemper, Delaware 25
- Kemper, James L. 24
- Kennard, Joel S. 61
- Kennedy, John B. G. 57
- Kenny Jr., Dennis 10, 16
- Kentucky Volunteer Battalion (US) 62
- Kerrigan, James E. 21
- Kershaw, Joseph B. 6, 23
- Keyes, Erasmus D. 18
- Kimball, Nathan 15, 39, 49
- King, John Gadsden 6
- Kirby, Edmund 20
- Kirkland, William W. 23
- Kneisley, James W. 44
- Korff, Hermann J. 37

L

- Lackland, Francis 25
- Lafayette Country Mounted Rifle Company 14
- Lander, Frederick W. 10
- Lane, James H. 35
- Langdon, Loomis L. 63
- Langen, Edward 52
- Lardiner, James L. 59
- Larned, Frank H. 34
- Latham, Henry Grey 25
- Lauman, Jacob G. 56
- Lawrence, Samuel C. 19
- Lay, John F. 25
- Leasure, Daniel 59
- Lee, Robert E. 40
- Lee, Stephen D. 40
- Lee, William H. F. 40
- Lee, William R. 54
- Lewis, Charles I. 9
- Lewis, Edward A. 53
- Lewis, Levin M. 45
- Lexington Home Guard Battery 43
- Lightfoot, Charles E. 27
- Lionberger, John H. 48
- Logan, John A. 56
- Logwood, Thomas H. 57
- Longenecker, Henry C. 21, 22
- Longstreet, James 23
- Loomis, Cyrus O. 15, 39, 49
- Loring, William W. 40
- Lothrop, Warren L. 12
- Louisiana (2nd Company, Washington Artillery Battalion) Battery 42
- <u>Louisiana (Washington Artillery) Artillery Battalion</u> 25
- Lowe, Aden L. 52
- Lowe, John W. 8, 37
- Lowry, Reigart B. 34
- Lyon, Nathaniel 12, 29
- Lyons, George 19
- Lytle, William H. 37

M

- MacDonald, Emmett 36, 46
- MacFarlane, Archibald A. 36, 45
- Mack, John G. 15
- Mack, Oscar A. 16, 37
- Mader, G. W. 64
- Maffit, John N. 61
- Magruder, John B. 11
- Major, James P. 13, 30, 44
- Maney, George 40
- Mansfield, Joseph J. 9
- Manson, Mahlon D. 15
- Manter, Francis H. 52
- Marks, Samuel F. 57
- Marmaduke, John S. 12, 66
- Marsh, Charles Carroll 52
- Marsh, Samuel 21
- Marshall, Charles A. 62
- Marshall, Thomas A. 43
- Marston, Gilman 19
- Marston, John 34
- Martin, Henry P. 19
- Martin, James B. 27, 67
- Martin, John D. 58
- Martin, John W. 14, 32, 36, 46
- Martin, Robert 7
- Martin, William 34
- Marye, Lawrence S. 40
- Mason, John S. 48
- Mason, Rodney 18
- Matheson, Roderick 21
- Matthews, Stanley 37
- McBride, John H. 31, 45
- McCalmont, John S. 67
- McCausland, John 9, 33, 38
- McClellan, George B. 15
- McClernand, John A. 56
- McConnell, Daniel 19
- McCook, Alexander M. 18
- McCook, Robert L. 15, 37
- McCown, James C. 14, 32, 36, 46
- McCown, John P. 57

McCulloch, Benjamin	30
McCulloch, Robert	45
McCunn, John H.	21
McDonald, Angus W.	48
McDonald, Edward C.	43
McDonald, Edward H.	48
McDowell, Irvin	18
McFarland, Walter	63
McGhee, Edward F.	58
McGinnis, A. B.	9
McIntosh, James M.	30
McKean, William	63
McLean, George W.	20
McLean, William	42
McMullin, James R.	37
McNairy, Frank N.	55
McRae, Dandridge	30
McRae, Duncan K.	24
Menken, Nathan D.	39
Mercer, Samuel	34
Meredith, Solomon	42
Meredith, Sullivan A.	21
Merrick, Thomas D.	58
Merritt, William H.	29
Metcalfe, Leonidas K.	62
Miles, Dixon S.	20, 21
Miller Jr., Matthew	20
Miller, Ezekiel S.	9
Miller, John	65
Miller, John H.	57
Miller, Merritt B.	25
Milroy, Robert H.	10, 15, 39, 49, 65
Minier, Francis P.	22
Mississippi (Pettus Flying Artillery) Battery	57
Mississippi (Point Coupee Artillery) Battery	58
Mississippi (Smith's) Battery	57
Mississippi (Warren Light Artillery) Battery	66
Mississippi (Watson) Battery	58
Missouri Cavalry Company	52
Missouri State Guard Artillery Battery (1st)	53
Missouri State Guard Battalion (4th)	44
Missouri State Guard Cavalry Battalion (4th)	44, 47
Mitchell, James K.	45
Mitchell, Robert B.	29
Monroe, Alexander	48
Montague, Edgar B.	11
Montgomery, James	35
Montgomery, William R.	20
Moody, Gideon C.	65
Mooney, James J.	54
Moor, Augustus	37
Moore, Henry	59
Moore, Lewis T.	25
Moore, Patrick T.	24
Moore, Sydenham	27
Moore, William H.	26
Moorman, Robert B.	40
Morris, Thomas A.	10, 15
Morrow, Isaac H.	15, 39
Morton, Thomas	16
Moss, John W.	39, 65
Mott, Christopher H.	27
Mott, Thaddeus P.	42
Mulligan, James A.	43, 44, 77
Munford, John D.	40
Murphy, John M.	21
Murphy, Robert C.	52
Murray, Thomas H.	31

N

Nagle, James	21
Napton, William	20
Neely, James J.	58
Neely, Rufus P.	58
Neff, George W.	8
Negley, James S.	22
Neibling, James M.	8
Nelson Rangers (Company B, 8th Virginia Cavalry)	33, 38
Newcomb, Henry S.	60
Newman, Tazewell W.	55
Nicholson, James W. A.	60
Nixon, Richard	34
Nobels, William H.	59
Norton, Jesse S.	8, 62

O

O'Kane, Walter S.	14, 36, 46
Oakford, Richard A.	22
Ord, Edward O. C.	67
Osterhaus, Peter J.	29
Owen, Joshua T.	22

P

Paine, Halbert E.	23
Palfrey, Francis W.	54
Palmer, Innis N.	19
Palmetto Guard	6
Palmyra Light Artillery Battery	44
Panabaker, William E.	52
Parker, Charles W.	7
Parrott, Enoch G.	60
Parsons, Mosby Monroe	13, 31, 45
Patrick, William	42
Patterson, Francis E.	22
Patterson, Robert	21
Patton Jr., John M.	40
Patton, George S.	8
Patton, Thomas Jefferson	44, 47
Payne, John W.	14, 32, 36, 46
Payne, William H. F.	25
Peabody, Everett	43

Peacher, Quinton L. 35, 44
Pearce, Nicholas B. 30
Peck, Henry W. 18
Pegram, John 16
Pelham, John 26, 73
Pelton, Frederick W. 15
Pendleton, William N. 26
Pennington, Alexander C. M. 63
Pennsylvania (Washington) Cavalry Company 49
Penrose, William H. 67
Perkins, Delevan D. 23
Perry, James H. 59
Pettigrew, James Johnston 7
Peyton, Robert L. Y. 14, 32, 36, 46
Pickett Jr., Edward 56
Pierce, Ebenezer W. 11
Pillow, Gideon J. 56
Pirner, Charles M. 43
Pittsylvania Cavalry 65
Pitzer, Andrew L. 67
Plummer, John B. 29, 52
Poindexter, John A. 44
Polk, Leonidas 56
Polk, Marshall T. 56
Porter, Andrew 19
Porterfield, George A. 10
Poschner, Frederick 37
Pratt, Calvin E. 21
Preston, James F. 25
Preston, Robert T. 24
Price, Edwin 35, 44
Price, Sterling 12, 30, 43, 44, 75, 77
Purcell, Charles W. 52

Q
Quinby, Isaac F. 18

R
Radford, Richard C. W. 25
Raine, Charles I. 65
Rains, James E. 55
Rains, James S. 13, 31, 35, 45
Ramsey, James N. 17, 41
Randolph, George W. 11
Rapley, William F. 53
Read, Jacob 61
Reger, Albert G. 10, 65
Reid, John G. 30
Reynolds, Alexander W. 33, 38
Reynolds, John G. 19
Reynolds, Joseph J. 39, 49
Reynolds, William H. 19, 23
Rhett, Alfred B. 7
Rice, Percy W. 10
Rice, William H. 41, 50
Rich, Lucius L. 58

Rich, Rishworth 59
Richardson, E. G. 53
Richardson, Israel B. 18
Richmond (1st) Howitzer Battalion 11
Ricketts, James B. 20
Rigby, Silas F. 39
Rigby's Indiana Battery 39
Riggins, George W. 44
Ripley, Roswell S. 7
Rives, Benjamin A. 13, 31, 44
Robertson, James M. 51, 63
Robinson, James W. 43
Robinson, John A. 49
Robinson, John H. 39, 49
Robinson, John M. 43
Robinson, O. O. G. 42
Rodes, Robert E. 23
Rogers, Arthur L. 25
Rogers, Christopher R. P. 59
Rosa, Rudolph 59
Rosecrans, William S. 15, 37
Ross, John D. H. 65
Ross, Leonard F. 52
Ross, William B. 56
Rosser, Thomas H. 14, 31, 36, 45
Rosser, Thomas L. 25, 42
Rowan, Samuel C. 34
Rowley, Thomas A. 22
Runyon, Theodore 20
Russell, Robert M. 56
Rust, Albert 40, 49
Rutledge Mounted Riflemen 7
Rutledge, Arthur M. 55
Rutledge, Benjamin H. 7

S
Salomon, Charles E. 13, 30
Sandy Rangers 9
Sanford, Charles W. 22
Saunders, James P. 44, 47
Savage, John H. 40
Scammon, Eliakim Parker 37
Schaefer, Frederick 12
Schaefer, Gustavus A. 30
Schaller, Frank 58
Schambeck, Frederick 37
Schenck, Robert C. 18
Schleich, Newton 15
Schneider, George 37
Schoepf, Albin F. 55
Schofield, John M. 52
Schutzenberg, Edward 30
Schwarzwaelder, Christian 22
Scott, John 47
Scott, Thomas M. 58

Scott, William C.	16, 41, 50
Screvens, John H.	61
Secrest, Andrew J.	67
Sedgwick, Thomas D.	8
Seeley, Francis W.	63
Seibels, John J.	23
Serrell, Edward W.	59
Seymour, Isaac G.	23
Seymour, Truman	6
Shaler, Alexander	42
Shawhan, Jonathan	62
Shelby, Joseph O.	14
Shepherd, Oliver L.	22
Sherman, Thomas W.	59
Sherman, William T.	18
Shields, James C.	25
Shipley, Alexander M.	51, 63
Shumaker, Lindsay M.	17, 41, 50
Sigel, Franz	13, 29
Sill, Joshua W.	62
Silloway, Jacob	63
Simmonds, Seth J.	8
Simmonds, William R.	15
Simons, James	6
Singleton, Middleton G.	35, 44
Skinner, Frederick G.	24
Slack, William Y.	13, 30, 44
Sloan, John B. E.	24
Slocum, Henry W.	19
Slocum, John S.	19
Slover, Thomas H.	32
Smith, Edmund Kirby	27
Smith, Francis J.	53
Smith, John G.	17
Smith, John J.	53
Smith, Melancthon	57
Smith, Preston	57
Smith, Robert A.	64
Smith, William	24
Smith, William F.	42
Smith, William Sooy	16, 37
Smyth Dragoons (Company A, 8th Virginia Cavalry)	33, 38
Sondershoff, Charles	15, 37
South Carolina (Beaufort Artillery) Battery	61
South Kansas-Texas Mounted Regiment	30
Stahel, Julius	21
Stanard, Philip B.	28
Stanard, Robert C.	11
Standart, William B.	55
Stanley, Timothy R.	16
Stannard, George J.	42
Staples, Henry G.	20
Starkweather, John C.	22
Statham, Winfield S.	55
Steedman, Charles	60
Steedman, James B.	10, 15, 55
Steele, Frederick	29
Steen, Alexander E.	35, 44
Stellwagen, Henry S.	34
Stembel, Roger N.	56
Stephens, William H.	57
Sterling, Robert	58
Sterrett, Franklin P.	16
Steuart, George H.	27
Stevens, Isaac I.	42, 59
Stevens, Peter F.	6
Stevens, Thomas H.	60
Stewart, Alexander P.	58
Stewart, Richard A.	58
Stewart, Warren	52
Stiles Jr., William H.	60
Stiles, John W.	22
Stone, Charles P.	22
Strahl, Otho F.	58
Strange, John B.	24
Strickland, Lee	59
Stringham, Silas H.	34
Stuart, Hal M.	61
Stuart, James E. B.	28, 42, 67
Stuart, William D.	11
Stumbaugh, Frederick S.	22
Sturges, Stephen B.	10
Sturgis, Samuel D.	29
Sullivan, Jeremiah C.	15, 39, 49, 65
Swett, Charles M.	66
Sykes, George	19
T	
Taggart, John H.	67
Taliaferro, Alexander G.	41, 50
Taliaferro, William B.	17, 41, 50
Tappan, James C.	57
Tappan, Mason	22
Tattnall, Josiah	61
Taylor, Ezra	56
Taylor, Franck E.	51
Taylor, George W.	20
Taylor, Thomas H.	26, 67
Tennessee (Bankhead's [Company B, 1st Tennessee Light Artillery]) Battery	57
Tennessee (Company E, 1st Tennessee Heavy Artillery) Battery	58
Tennessee (Company F, 1st Tennessee Heavy Artillery) Battery	58
Tennessee (Jackson's) Battery	56
Tennessee (Memphis Light) Battery	58
Tennessee (Polk's) Battery	56
Tennessee (Rutledge's) Battery	55

Tennessee (Southern Guards Artillery [Memphis Southern Guards Artillery]) ...57
Terrett, George H. ...23
Terrill, James B. ...42
Terry, Alfred H. ...18, 59
Terry, Benjamin F. ...66
Terry, William R. ...24
Thayer, S. C. ...7
Thomas, George H. ...21
Thomas, John P. ...6
Thompson, George H. ...50
Thompson, John H. ...33, 38
Thompson, Meriwether Jefferson ...52
Thornton, John C. C. ...13, 31, 35, 45
Thornton, William W. ...25
Tidball, John C. ...21
Tompkins, Christopher Q. ...8, 33, 37
Tompkins, George W. B. ...18
Totten, James ...12, 29
Townsend, Frederick ...11
Travis, William E. ...57
Trumbull, Matthew M. ...47
Tupper, Samuel Y. ...7
Turley, John A. ...16
Turney, Peter ...27
Twigg, Brigham F. ...45
Tyler, Daniel ...18
Tyler, Erastus B. ...15, 33
Tyree, William ...9

U
U.S. Reserve Corps Infantry Battalion ...43
U.S.S. Adelaide ...34
U.S.S. Augusta ...60
U.S.S. Bienville ...60
U.S.S. Cumberland ...34
U.S.S. Curlew ...60
U.S.S. Fanny ...34
U.S.S. George Peabody ...34
U.S.S. Hartford [Richmond] ...63
U.S.S. Isaac Smith ...60
U.S.S. Lexington ...56
U.S.S. Minnesota ...34
U.S.S. Mohican ...59
U.S.S. Monticello ...34
U.S.S. Niagara ...63
U.S.S. Ottawa ...60
U.S.S. Pawnee ...34, 60
U.S.S. Pembina ...60
U.S.S. Penguin ...60
U.S.S. Pocahontas ...59
U.S.S. R.B. Forbes ...60
U.S.S. Seminole ...60
U.S.S. Seneca ...60
U.S.S. Susquehanna ...34, 59
U.S.S. Tyler ...56
U.S.S. Unadilla ...60
U.S.S. Vanadalia ...60
U.S.S. Wabash ...34, 59
United States Infantry Battalion ...19
United States Marine Corps Battalion ...19
Utterback, Robert E. ...25

V
Van Benthuysen, Alfred C. ...64
Van Brunt, Gershom J. ...34
Van Horn, Robert T. ...43
Vaughan, Joseph ...44
Vaughn, John C. ...27
Viele, Egbert L. ...59
Villepigue, John B. ...64
Virginia (1st Company, Richmond Howitzers) Battery ...25
Virginia (1st Rockbridge Artillery) Battery ...26
Virginia (2nd Rockbridge Artillery) Battery ...65
Virginia (8th Star Artillery) Battery ...41, 50
Virginia (Alexandria Artillery) Battery ...25
Virginia (Danville Artillery) Battery ...17, 41, 50
Virginia (Gauley Artillery) Battery ...33, 38
Virginia (Goochland Artillery) Battery ...33, 38
Virginia (Hampden Artillery) Battery ...40
Virginia (Kanawha Artillery) Battery ...9, 33, 38
Virginia (Latham) Artillery ...24
Virginia (Latham) Battery ...25
Virginia (Loudoun Artillery) Battery ...25
Virginia (Lynchburg "Lee" Artillery) Battery 17, 41, 50, 65
Virginia (Newtown Artillery) Battery ...27
Virginia (Purcell Artillery) Battery ...25
Virginia (Staunton Artillery) Battery ...27
Virginia (Thomas Artillery) Battery ...28
Virginia (Wise Artillery) Battery ...26
Vodges, Israel ...51
Voerster, John D. ...29
Von Gilsa, Leopold ...20
Von Steinwehr, Adolph W. ...21
Von Trebra, Henry ...66

W
Wagner, George D. ...15, 39, 49
Wagoner, John A. ...61
Walke, Henry ...56
Walker, Benjamin F. ...14, 32, 36, 46
Walker, James D. ...30
Walker, Joseph Knox ...56
Walker, Reuben Lindsay ...25
Wallace, Lewis ...23
Walrath, Ezra L. ...18
Walton, James B. ...25
Ward, John Henry Hobart ...20
Washburn, Peter ...11
Watmaugh, Pendleton G. ...60
Watts, Thomas H. ...64

Waugh, Alexander	52
Webb, Robert F.	27
Weber, Max	34
Weer, William A.	35
Weightman, Richard H.	13, 31
West, William A.	37
Wharton, Gabriel C.	33, 38
Wheat, Chatham Roberdeau	24
Wheat, J. T.	64
Wheaton, Frank	19
Whipple, Thomas J.	59
White, Carr B.	37
White, James D.	53
White, John R.	44
White, Patrick H.	52
White, Percy W.	16
White, Robert	43
Whiting, Henry	20
Whiting, William H. C.	26
Whittemore, Horace O.	11
Wickham, Williams C.	25
Wilcox, Cadmus M.	27
Wilfley, Redmond	45, 47
Wilkins, Theodore	13
Willcox, Orlando B.	20
Williams, Adolphus W.	18
Williams, Edward C.	21
Williams, James H.	23
Williams, John S.	62
Williams, William O.	58
Williams, William S.	8
Willich, August	66
Wilson, William	51
Wingo, Edmund T.	31, 45
Winston, John A.	27
Winston, John H.	45, 47
Wise, Henry A.	8
Wise, Obadiah Jennings	9, 33, 38
Wistar, Isaac J.	54
Withers, Robert E.	24
Wolff, Christian D.	13
Wolford, Frank	55
Wood, Alfred M.	19
Woodbury, Dwight A.	20
Woodhouse, Levi	22
Woodruff Jr., William E.	30
Woodruff, William E.	8
Woods, Samuel B.	9
Wright, Clark	29
Wright, Horatio G.	59
Wright, John V.	56
Wright, Marcus J.	57
Wyman, Robert H.	60
Wynkoop, George C.	22

Y

Yohe, Samuel	22

Z

Zeigler, Thomas A.	22
Zolicoffer, Felix K.	55

Printed in Great Britain
by Amazon